the Covenants

edenic

adamic

noahic

abrahamic

mosaic

the Covenants

palestinian

davidic

new

everlasting

Kevin Conner & Ken Malmin

Published by City Bible Publishing
9200 NE Fremont
Portland, Oregon 97220

Printed in U.S.A.

City Bible Publishing is a ministry of City Bible Church, and is dedicated to serving the local church and its leaders through the production and distribution of quality materials.

It is our prayer that these materials, proven in the context of the local church, will equip leaders in exalting the Lord and extending His kingdom.

For a free catalog of additional resources from City Bible Publishing please call 1-800-777-6057 or visit our web site at www.citybiblepublishing.com.

The Covenants
© Copyright 1983 by Bible Temple Publishing
All Rights Reserved

Updated and Revised 1997

ISBN 0-914936-77-8
Australian ISBN 0-949829-02-1

CONTENTS

FOREWORD

The Preacher said "All the rivers run into the sea; yet the sea is not full; unto the place from whence the rivers come, thither they return again" (Ecclesiastes 1:7). The Psalmist said "There is *a river, the streams* whereof shall make glad the city of God, the holy place of the tabernacles of the Most High" (Psalms 46:4). The more a believer studies the Word of God, the more he discovers the truth of both the Preacher's and the Psalmist's words.

Symbolically there are rivers of truth and revelation which begin in the Book of Genesis and flow on in deepening, widening and refreshing glory into the sea of fulfilment, the Book of Revelation.

Through many years of studying that inexhaustible Book called the Bible, believers have discovered many streams of truth. However, there is a deep vast river, a mainstream of revelation, which flows through God's Word. This mainstream is the flow of God's ongoing covenantal revelation. It actually began, as all rivers do, in the mountain of God's eternal purposes concerning man. Then, under the melting sunlight of God's love and grace it began to flow down to earth. It has been flowing on and on, through the Edenic, Adamic, Noahic, Abrahamic, Mosaic, Palestinian, Davidic and New Covenants. The New Covenant brings the river of covenantal revelation into the sea of fulfilment and thus the river returns to the place from whence it came. Moses saw the river in Genesis parting into its four heads to bless the earth (Genesis 2:10-14). John then saw the river in the city of God on a great and high mountain (Revelation 21:9,10; 22:1-3). The cycle of covenantal revelation which was in the Everlasting Covenant is now complete.

There are many streams of truth in the Word of God; theological, prophetical, typical, symbolical, eschatological and practical. However, all of these streams of truth flow out of and back into the mainstream of covenantal truth. None of these "streams" are the total river and it is dangerous to believe that any one of them is the whole river of Divine revelation. All streams must flow out of and back into the river of God. This river is the covenantal truth which flows from Genesis through the 66 books of the Bible into Revelation.

In *"The Covenants"* there are "waters to swim in" and one may go ankle deep, knee deep, to the waist or find a river that cannot be passed over (Ezekiel 47:1-12). The covenantal river is full of water that one can be enriched thereby (Psalms 65:9-10). Here the believer may drink of the river of God's pleasures (Psalms 36:8).

The word "covenant" is a word that has lost its meaning and significance in present society. In Bible times the word "covenant" involved promise, commitment, faithfulness and loyalty even unto death. A covenant was sacred and was not lightly entered into by the parties involved. In Bible times a person was only as good as their covenant word. In a society where national agreements, business contracts, and marriage covenants are under stress and attack, where people are "covenant-breakers" (Romans 1:31), it brings great joy and comfort to know that God is a covenant-making and covenant-keeping God.

True believers are in covenant relationship with God through Christ and the New Covenant. They are also in covenant relationship with each other. This is symbolized each time believers meet together around the Lord's Table, the New Covenant table. There they partake of the broken body and shed blood of the covenant Christ of God. What a spiritual transformation would come to the Church if believers would understand, appreciate and experience covenantal relationship and commitment!

It is to this end that *"The Covenants"* textbook has been written.

Our prayer is that Ministers, Students and all believers who read and study this text will receive that illumination and flow into the river of God's covenantal revelation in true commitment to Christ and to the members of His New Covenant Body, which is the Church.

Kevin J. Conner
Kenneth P. Malmin

(NOTE: Unless otherwise stated, Scripture References are taken from King James Version of the Bible.)

Chapter 1

AN INTRODUCTION TO THE COVENANTS

The Bible reveals that God is a covenant-making, covenant-keeping and covenant-revealing God. The Bible itself is a covenantal book being divided into two sections, the Old and New Testaments (Covenants), and containing a progressive revelation of nine major covenants. These Covenants comprise the purposes of God in both Creation and Redemption and involve time and eternity. One of the primary keys to the interpretation of Scripture is the Covenantal Principal of Hermeneutics.

I. **What Is A Covenant?**

In modern society the word *"covenant"* has lost some of the fulness and richness that it had in Bible times. In order to rediscover its meaning we will consider its definitions in English, Hebrew and Greek.

A. **English**

In English the word "covenant" signifies a mutual understanding between two or more parties, each binding himself to fulfill specified obligations; a legal contract; a binding agreement; a written agreement. It also refers to a solemn agreement to do or not to do a certain thing.

B. **Old Testament Hebrew**

Strong's Concordance defines the Hebrew word Beriyth as "a compact (because made by passing between pieces of flesh)" which implies the thought of cutting a covenant (Genesis 15:17; Jeremiah 34:18).

Gesenius defines this word as "a covenant, pact or compact." He then expands this by giving a number of applied definitions under the following categories:

1. **Between men**
   a. treaty, alliance, league (Genesis 14:13; Exodus 23:32; 34:12,15, Joshua 9:6-16).
   b. constitution, ordinance (between monarch & subjects) (II Samuel 3:12,13; 5:3, Jeremiah 34:8-18).
   c. agreement, pledge (II Kings 11:4; Hosea 10:4).
   d. alliance of friendship (I Samuel 18:3; 20:8; 23:18).
   e. alliance of marriage (Proverbs 2:17; Malachi 2:14).

2. **Between God and man**
   a. alliance of friendship (Psalms 25:14).
   b. covenant, as a divine constitution or ordinance with signs or pledges (Genesis 9:9-17; Exodus 2:24).

3. **Phrases**

    a.   covenant-making (Genesis 15:18; Exodus 34:10,17).

    b.   covenant-keeping (I Kings 11:11; Leviticus 26:42).

    c.   covenant violation (Deuteronomy 17:2; Leviticus 26:15,44).

In the *King James Version* Beriyth is translated; confederacy (Genesis 14:13; Obadiah 7), league (Joshua 9:6,7; Judges 2:2) and covenant (Genesis 6:18; Leviticus 2:13; Psalms 89:3,4; Daniel 9:27).

C.   New Testament Greek

In the New Testament there are two Greek words for covenant. Diatheke means "a disposition, arrangement, testament or will".

According to *Arndt and Gingrich's Lexicon* this word means:

> "1. last will and testament. (so exclusively in Hellenistic times) . . . a will that has been ratified, Galatians 3:15 . . . in extra-Biblical sources, namely 'decree', 'declaration of purpose' . . . The declaration of one person's will, not the result of an agreement between parties, like a compact or contract . . . The meaning compact, contract seems to be established for classical times."

Moulton and Milligan add that:

> ". . . diatheke is properly disposition, an 'arrangement' made by one party with plenary power, which the other party may accept or reject, but cannot alter."

In the *King James Version* Diatheke is translated: testament (Matthew 26:28; Hebrews 7:22; 9:15-17,20; Revelation 11:19) and covenant (Luke 1:72; Romans 9:14; Ephesians 2:12; Hebrews 12:14; 13:20).

The other Greek word, Suntithemai, means "to put together, place together, to make arrangement." It refers to an arrangement between men and is never used to refer to the covenants made by God and presented to man. In the King James version it is translated: covenanted (Luke 22:5), agreed (John 9:22; Acts 23:20) and assented (Acts 24:9).

The word "covenant" in Scripture refers to an agreement or a contract between men, or between God and man. In Scripture, we find that men often made covenants with men in relation to various matters (e.g., Genesis 21:27,31,32 — covenant between Abraham and Abimelech concerning the well of Beersheba; Luke 22:5 — covenant between the chief priests and Judas concerning the price of betrayal).

In every case in Scripture when a covenant was instituted between God and man, God is seen as the initiator. Man did not come to God with a proposal seeking God's approval, rather God came to man declaring His will and seeking man's adherence. A covenant is a contract between God and man drawn up by God and presented to man. Man can either accept it or reject it, but he cannot change it. However, the usage of "covenant" in Scripture does not always contain the idea of joint obligation, but may signify an obligation undertaken by a single person: God. In these instances, the aspect of covenant is emphasized in "the promise" (Galatians 3:17; Romans 15:8).

II.   **Who Originated The Covenants?**

Being an interpersonal arrangement a covenant must be made by one person for or with another. The covenants between God and man had to originate with God for He alone has the mind, authority and ability to make them effective. It was always His heart and nature that motivated Him to initiate the covenants with man. The covenants are the greatest manifestations of God's love, grace and mercy.

A.   **A Covenant-Making God**

God established His covenant with Noah (Genesis 6:18). He made a covenant with Abraham (Genesis 15:18; 17:2). God made a covenant with David (II Samuel 23:5). He promised to make a new covenant with the House of Israel and the House of Judah (Jeremiah 31:31-34). He has also made an everlasting covenant (Isaiah 55:3; 61:8).

B.   **A Covenant-Keeping God**

God reveals His faithfulness and trustworthiness in that He keeps the covenant that He makes. Once God has made a covenant He does not forget it nor become negligent of it. He always follows through with the commitments He has made (Deuteronomy 7:9; II Chronicles 6:14; Psalms 111:5,9; Romans 1:31).

C.   **A Covenant-Revealing God**

In order for man to be in covenant relationship with God He must reveal the covenant to man, openly declaring the promises and terms. Apart from God taking the initiative and revealing His covenant to man, man would be ignorant of the availability of covenantal relationship with Him (Psalms 25:14; Deuteronomy 4:13).

D.   **A Covenant-Enabling God**

The same God who makes, keeps and reveals His covenants to man also enables man to fulfill his part of the covenant. Apart from the enabling grace of God man has proven his inability to keep the terms of any covenant. This was particularly illustrated under the Mosaic Covenant (Ephesians 2:4-13).

III.   **Why Make A Covenant?**

The general purpose for a covenant is to provide a binding sense of commitment to an interpersonal relationship. The binding force of even human covenants is seen in Joshua's covenant with the Gibeonites (Joshua 9:1-27; II Samuel 21) and in Zedekiah's covenant with Nebuchadnezzar (Jeremiah 34:8-18; Ezekiel 17:11-21). Those who enter into covenant obligate themselves to that relationship and provide it with a strong sense of security. This is vividly illustrated in the marriage covenant which was instituted by God to be a model of His covenants. God hates divorce because it disannuls a covenant, destroys its very purpose and does not accurately reflect the irrevocability of the covenants by which man is redeemed (Malachi 2:14-16).

The specific purpose of the Divine covenants is for them to be the vehicles of the expression of God's will and purpose for man. They are also to be the effective means by which His will and purpose is fulfilled.

God has a reason for everything He does. He moves with definite purpose. Careful forethought and planning goes into all His works. All of God's purposes proceed from His person. What He does is always consistent with who He is. The kind of person He is dictates the kind of things He does (Isaiah 14:26,27; Romans 8:28; Isaiah 14:14,27; II Timothy 1:9; Isaiah 46:11; Ephesians 1:9-11; 3:9-11).

God's purpose for man is seen in both creation and redemption. Before the fall of man God expressed His purpose in creating man in the form of a covenant: the Edenic Covenant. The fulfilment of this covenant was interrupted and apparently frustrated by Adam's breaking of the conditions of that covenant. This necessitated and ushered in the expression of God's redemptive purpose for man in the form of the redemptive covenants: the Adamic, Noahic, Abrahamic, Mosaic, Palestinian, Davidic and New Covenants. Thus there was a covenant of creation and covenants of redemption. All of these were included in the scope of the Everlasting Covenant which is the most comprehensive expression of both God's creative and redemptive purposes for man.

IV.   **What Constitutes A Covenant?**

In keeping with the threeness of God's person, there is also a threeness to the expressions of His purpose. Each Divine covenant has basically three parts to it. These are:

* The *Words* or Promises of the Covenant.

* The *Blood* of the Covenant.

* The *Seal* of the Covenant.

Any covenant is incomplete and therefore invalid without the testimony of these three things. Thus the triune God gave triune covenants. Each person in the Godhead, Father, Son and Holy Spirit, had a part in the making, ratifying and sealing of the covenants. In this way the characteristics of the Godhead were impressed on the covenants, as the following chart illustrates.

THE FATHER	THE SON	THE HOLY SPIRIT
The originator, initiator, covenant-maker and keeper, the source, the first, the beginning.	The sacrifice of body and blood, the second person, the mediator and ratifier of the covenant.	The executor appointed to carry out the will and testament of the Father and the Son, the third person, the completor and fulfiller of the covenant
THE WORDS/ PROMISES of the Covenant	THE BLOOD of the Covenant	THE SEAL of the Covenant
The Father's Word To Us	The Son's Work For Us	The Holy Spirit's Work In Us

A. **The Words Of The Covenant**

In that a covenant is an expressed agreement it consists of words that are either verbalized or written. Involved in the words of each covenant are its promises and terms, as well as the possibility of an oath and a book.

1. The *Promises* of the Covenant

    In that a covenant is an interpersonal commitment the persons involved would most likely express that commitment in the form of a promise. These promises, could include:

    a. Promises of blessing.

    b. Promises of cursing.

    c. Natural, national and temporal promises.

    d. Spiritual and eternal promises.

2. The *Terms* of the Covenant

    Any agreement between two parties of necessity involves certain conditions under which the promises will be fulfilled on the part of the covenantor and/or the covenantee.

3. The *Oath* of the Covenant

    Certain of the Divine Covenants have their promises confirmed with an oath. When such is the case the covenant become irrevocable. Without an oath the promises may be subject to change or cancellation.

    a. **Definition of the word**

        (1) **Dictionary**

            "A solemn affirmation with an appeal to God for its truth."

            *   Oath-breaking = violation of an oath; perjury.

            *   Oath of Allegiance = an oath binding to true allegiance to a specified power.

            *   Oath of Supremacy = an oath declaring and establishing the supremacy of British sovereigns over every other power, spiritual or temporal in their realm.

        (2) **Hebrew**

            SHEBOOAW — Something sworn; an oath, a curse. Signifies "to be complete; to seven oneself, i.e., swear (as if by repeating a declaration seven times)".

        (3) **Greek**

            HORKOS — A fence, a limit, a sacred restraint placed on oneself. Together these words show that the oath is a solemn affirmation. It is the giving of one's word which binds them to its fulfilment. An oath attached to any covenant promise makes it irrevocable, unable to be annulled.

    b. **Illustration of the word**

        Following are several illustrations from the Scripture which show how the oath makes a covenant irrevocable and binding, never to be made null and void.

(1) People made promises and then added an oath to assure another person that they would keep their promises. Joseph took oath of his sons concerning his bones (Genesis 50:25), (Joshua 2:17,20; 9:18-20).

(2) The oath and the promise bound the one who uttered it to its fulfilment (Numbers 30:2,10; I Samuel 14:26-28; Acts 23:21; II Chronicles 6:22; 15:15).

(3) In certain cases, only a person in authority could release someone from an unwise oath and promise (Genesis 24:8,41; Numbers 30:2,10,13).

(4) The oath made covenant promises irrevocable, so that they could never be annulled (Matthew 14:9; Genesis 26:23,33; Jeremiah 11:5; Zechariah 8:17).

(5) To break an oath was to inflict a curse upon oneself (Nehemiah 5:12; 10:29; Ezekiel 16:59; Daniel 9:11; Numbers 5:19-25).

When God made promises and confirmed them with an oath, He bound Himself to their fulfilment, making the covenant irrevocable. Such is seen in the Noahic Covenant (Isaiah 54:9), the Abrahamic Covenant (Hebrews 6:16-17), and the Davidic Covenant (Psalms 89:3,35; 132:11), which consummates in the New Covenant with Christ after the order of Melchisedek (Acts 2:30; Psalms 110; Hebrews 7:20,21,28). God's oath to His promises is a confirmation and an end of all strife and unbelief on the part of man.

4.   The *Book* of the Covenant

Though all the Divine covenants were eventually put into written form the only one that was specifically made into a book of its own was the Mosaic covenant which was expressly called "The book of the covenant" (Exodus 24:7). The other covenants ended up being recorded in the greatest "Book of the Covenant" which is the Bible.

B.   **The Blood of the Covenant**

In that a covenant was viewed as being a life and death commitment the ratification of it involved bloodshed. The sacrificial blood used to make the covenant official represented the life commitment of those entering into the covenant. In that a covenant was substantiated by sacrifice it necessitated a priest to offer the sacrifice as well as a sanctuary in which the priest could function.

1.   The *Sacrifice* of the Covenant

Covenantal sacrifice involved both the shedding of blood and the death of the body. This solemn act vividly illustrated the sacredness of the covenant vows. The sacrifice involved both:

a.   The Body

b.   The Blood

2. The *Mediator* of the Covenant

    Any sacrifice necessitates a sacrificer, one who is a mediator officiating the covenant ratification ceremony. This would include:

    a. The Mediator and High Priest.

    b. The Priesthood.

3. The *Sanctuary* of the Covenant

    A holy act must occur in a holy place. There must be a place for the functioning of the priesthood in the ministry of the covenant. This involved:

    a. The Altar.

    b. The Tabernacle or Temple.

C. The Seal of the Covenant

A seal is an ongoing tangible witness to the veracity of the covenant. It serves as a constant reminder of the authenticity of the covenantal promises and terms. Each of the Divine Covenants had its own particular seal which was referred to as either:

1. The Seal of the Covenant.

2. The Sign of the Covenant, or

3. The Token of the Covenant.

V. What Is The Duration Of A Covenant?

Any covenant or agreement made between men may either have a period of time stated concerning its duration or may be stated as being in effect indefinitely. The Divine covenants were made to be either everlasting or temporal. Some were meant to be in effect for a certain period of time while others were made to be in effect for time and eternity. This is related to the fact that some covenants were revocable while others were irrevocable.

A. Everlasting Covenants

Certain of the Divine covenants were expressly spoken of as "everlasting covenants" (Genesis 9:16; 17:13; Numbers 25:12,13; II Samuel 23:5; Ezekiel 16:60; Hebrews 13:20). These covenants were made to be never ending, eternal, perpetual, and age-abiding. They were to continue to be in effect forever. However, in the promises, sacrifices and seals of these everlasting covenants there were elements that could not last forever because of their temporal nature. For example, the Abrahamic Covenant is spoken of an everlasting covenant and the seal of it, which is circumcision, is also spoken of as being everlasting (Genesis 17:13). However, the New Testament declares that the external expression of the seal, the circumcision of the flesh, was fulfilled and abolished at the cross. Therefore only the internal and spiritual reality of the seal, which is circumcision of the heart, can be everlasting. Likewise, the animal sacrifices of the everlasting covenants could never be eternal. Only through the once-for-all sacrifice of the Son of God could the principle of covenantal sacrifice be everlasting though the external form was fulfilled and abolished (Genesis 15; Hebrews 10). Though having temporal elements everlasting covenants are legally binding and remain in effect for eternity.

B. **Temporal Covenants**

Other of the Divine covenants were shown to be temporal (Galatians 3:19; Hebrews 9:10). They were made to be limited to time and not permanent. Perhaps the greatest illustration of this was the Mosaic covenant. The Tabernacle services, the sacrificial system, the priesthood, and the festival occasions comprised an external and temporal form of the law. These temporal elements continued to be in effect until Christ fulfilled and abolished them. However the spiritual knowledge and truth contained in the form is eternal and remains forever (Romans 2:20). Though having eternal and spiritual implications temporal covenants are legally limited to a certain period of time.

C. **Irrevocable Covenants**

An irrevocable covenant is one in which God obligates Himself to fulfill the promises of the covenant regardless of man's response. It remains in effect whether or not man is fulfilling the conditions of it. The strength of an irrevocable covenant is found in the key words "I will". Following are two examples:

1. **The Abrahamic Covenant**

God promised Abraham "I will multiply thy seed as the stars of the heaven, and as the sand which is upon the sea shore . . ." (Genesis 22:17). Though in the context of this promise the obedience of Abraham is referred to there is no mention of his seed needing to remain obedient in order for this covenant promise to remain in effect. Abraham's seed was to be innumerable as the stars and sand regardless of their goodness or wickedness.

2. **The Davidic Covenant**

God promised David "I will set up thy seed after thee . . . and I will establish his kingdom." (II Samuel 7:12) This promise guaranteed David that there would always be one of his descendants sitting upon his throne. There is no mention of their obedience as a condition for the promise to remain in effect. In reference to their disobedience God did promise "If he commit iniquity, I will chasten him with the rod of men . . . but my mercy shall not depart away . . ." (II Samuel 7:14,15). Regardless of the goodness or wickedness of the Davidic kings this covenant promise would remain irrevocable.

D. **Revocable Covenants**

A revocable covenant is one in which God obligates Himself to fulfill the promises of the covenant only upon man's obedience to the conditions attached to it by God. If the covenant is broken by man God is not obligated to fulfill His part and it is dissolved, disannulled and no longer remains in effect. This is particularly illustrated in the Mosaic covenant. God stated to Jeremiah concerning this covenant "which my covenant they brake" (Jeremiah 31:32). He also told Zechariah "that I might break my covenant which I had made with all the people." (Zechariah 11:10) Paul spoke of this covenant as being abolished

(II Corinthians 3:13), decaying, waxing old and ready to vanish away (Hebrews 8:13). All these terms serve to confirm the revocability of the Mosaic Covenant.

VI. How Is Covenant Relationship Established?

In order for covenant relationship to be established both parties must understand and fulfill their part of the covenant agreement. The one initiating the covenant must make it available and the one receiving the covenant must respond by entering into and maintaining its terms.

A. By Calling

God initiated each covenant by first formulating it and then offering it to man, inviting man to come into that covenant relationship. Calling means to invite or bid to come to one's self (Romans 8:28-30; II Timothy 1:9). In the covenants God calls and bids man to come to Himself. It is God's prerogative to offer His covenants to whoever He chooses. These who were chosen to receive God's covenants were called to enter into them (Nehemiah 9:7-8; Acts 7:1-8; Hebrews 11:8-10; Genesis 12:1-3).

B. By Entering

How can man receive and enjoy the benefits of the covenants that God initiates? Is it only by God's choice or does man have a part? Scripture clearly reveals that man must "enter into covenant" (Deuteronomy 29:1,12; II Chronicles 15:12; Jeremiah 34:10), and that he must "take hold of the covenant" (Isaiah 56:4,6).

In that God Himself enters into a covenant (Ezekiel 16:8), He can require man to enter into that covenant (Deuteronomy 29:12). Man cannot do what only God can do but God will not do what man must do. Man has the responsibility to commit himself fully to the covenant that God calls him into. This he does by faith and obedience (Hebrews 11:8). Israel failed to enter into the covenant land because of unbelief and disobedience (Hebrews 3-4; Luke 11:52; John 6:28,29).

C. By Keeping

God is a covenant-keeping God and thus requires man to "keep the covenant" (Deuteronomy 29:9; 33:9; Psalms 103:17-18). To keep the covenant is to remember it and to continually fulfill its terms. This God does (Psalms 111:5; Genesis 9:15,16), and so must man (Psalms 103:18). The way covenantal relationship is entered into is also the way it is maintained: by faith and obedience (Hebrews 4:11; 5:9; Genesis 22:18; 26:5; Exodus 19:5; Deuteronomy 11:27; 30:6-8; Jeremiah 7:22-28; 11:1-10; Romans 5:12-21). It is possible for man to break his covenantal relationship with God (Jeremiah 31:32; Hebrews 8:9).

SUMMARY

God, as the initiator of the covenants, has the perogative to set the conditions by which man may enter into and maintain his covenantal relationship.

VII. What Covenants Did God Make With Man?

Of the nine major Divine covenants in the Bible, eight of them God made with man. These are as follows:

1.   The Edenic Covenant

2.   The Adamic Covenant

3.   The Noahic Covenant

4.   The Abrahamic Covenant

5.   The Mosaic Covenant

6.   The Palestinian Covenant

7.   The Davidic Covenant

8.   The New Covenant

The Everlasting Covenant, the ninth covenant to be dealt with in this text, is that covenant made in the eternal counsels and persons of the Godhead. The covenants listed above were made with various individuals and peoples through various periods of human history as the following Scriptures reveal.

1.   **The Edenic Covenant** — made before the entrance of sin, involving the original man and woman, Adam and Eve. It reveals God's original purpose for the whole of Adam's race (Genesis 1-2).

2.   **The Adamic Covenant** — made after the entrance of sin, with Adam and Eve, the original sinners and parents of the human race. It involved God's judgment on sin and the coming of Messianic redemption (Genesis 3).

3.   **The Noahic Covenant** — made with Noah, after the Flood, involving all creation, all creatures and all future generations of the human race. It re-establishes God's purpose as revealed in the Edenic Covenant (Genesis 6-9).

4.   **The Abrahamic Covenant** — made with Abraham, the father of all who believe, the father of the chosen nation of Israel, after the Tower of Babel and the scattering of the sons of Noah in their tongues, families and nations. It involved Abraham, his natural and national seed called Israel and the Messianic seed, Jesus Christ. It includes in itself the coming in of the believing Israelites and Gentiles into the Kingdom of God (Genesis 12-22).

5.   **The Mosaic Covenant** — made strictly and only with the chosen nation of Israel, after the Exodus from Egypt at the foot of Mt Sinai. It was not made with any Gentile nation but acted as a "schoolmaster" to bring Israel to the Christ who would be the Saviour of the world (Galatians 3:24; Exodus 19-40).

6.   **The Palestinian Covenant** — made with the nation of Israel, especially the second and new generation at the end of the 40 years wanderings in the wilderness and before they entered Canaan, the land promised in the Abrahamic Covenant. It laid out the conditions for entering into and maintaining the promised land (Deuteronomy 27-33).

7.   **The Davidic Covenant** — made with David after the death of King Saul and at the establishment of the Kingdom of Israel under a Davidic King. It involved David, both his natural and spiritual seed and pointed ultimately to the Lord Jesus Christ and the everlasting throne and kingdom of the King of kings and Lord of lords (II Samuel 7; Psalms 89; Psalms 132).

8. **The New Covenant** — made with the two houses of Israel
    judicial rejection of Messiah by Jewry and just prior to
    replaced the Old or Mosaic Covenant with its external and
    and carnal ordinances. It made available through the cross
    whole world (Jeremiah 31:31-34; Hebrews 8; Matthew 26).

9. **The Everlasting Covenant** — made in eternity in the counsels of the eternal
    Godhead, between the Father, Son and Holy Spirit. It is the all-comprehensive
    covenant, including in itself the covenants of creation and redemption and
    God's eternal purpose for man. All other covenants are but fragments of the
    whole and are a progressive unfolding of this Everlasting Covenant.

VIII. How Are The Covenants Inter-related?

Because the covenants of God to man are but fragments of the whole and each are
part of the progressive revelation, there is inter-relatedness between them. They are
interwoven together from beginning to end.

The Edenic Covenant, in one sense, stands alone and unique, for it is the only
covenant involving man before the entrance of sin. It is the covenant which distinctly
declares God's purpose in the creation of man. The entrance of sin seemed to
frustrate the plan and purpose of God for man. However, God foresaw the fall of
man and was prepared for it. He immediately set into motion a series of covenants
revealing the plan of redemption. It would therefore be by the covenants of
redemption that the covenant of creation would find fulfilment. God would not
allow sin to annul His creative purposes for man as in the Edenic Covenant.

The first two covenants of redemption were the Adamic and Noahic Covenants.
Both were vitally linked as the covenantal language of each reveals. Both were given
to the Patriarchs; the first to Adam the father of the whole human race, and the next
to Noah the father of the race after the Flood. The major promises of these
covenants are that which spoke of redemption by the Messianic seed. Also in the
Noahic Covenant particularly the creative purpose of God as stated in the Edenic
Covenant is confirmed.

Arising out of the Adamic and Noahic Covenants is the Abrahamic Covenant. It was
an extension and an amplification of the previous covenants. It included basically
that which was in these covenants. However, it prophesied of the chosen nation,
Israel, through whom the Messiah would come. Besides natural and national
promises for Israel, its greatest promise was that which concerned all the families of
the earth being blessed through the Messianic seed.

Two subsequent covenants were given, these being the Davidic and the New
Covenants. A study of these covenants show that they were actually a part of the
Abrahamic Covenant. The Davidic Covenant involves the kings of the House of
David, of the tribe of Judah. It is the full manifestation of the promise of kings as
given in the Abrahamic Covenant, consummating in the Lord Jesus Christ, the Son
of David who is King of kings and Lord of lords. The New Covenant is the fulfilment
and fullest expression of the promise in the Abrahamic Covenant concerning his
seed blessing all the nations of the earth. This includes both believing Israelites and
Gentiles coming into salvation through the Lord Jesus Christ.

The Davidic and the New Covenants were in the Abrahamic Covenant. The Adamic,
Noahic, Abrahamic, Davidic and New Covenants, as covenants of redemption, are all
inter-related and extensions and fulfilments of each other, consummating in the

New Covenant. These covenants of redemption were designed to bring man back to the fulfilment of the covenant of creation, the Edenic Covenant.

Two covenants that are vitally linked and interwoven together are the Mosaic and the Palestinian Covenants. These two covenants are unique in that they pertain strictly to the nation of Israel. The Mosaic Covenant was expressed in moral, civil and ceremonial laws which governed the life of the people of Israel. The Palestinian Covenant pertained to the laws and conditions for Israel's living in the land of Canaan.

An analysis of the Mosaic and Palestinian Covenants reveals their link with the Abrahamic Covenant. Involved in the Abrahamic Covenant were promises concerning Abraham's seed and that seed's possessing of the promised land. The Mosaic Covenant concerned *the people,* the seed of Abraham. The Palestinian Covenant concerned *the land* promised in the Abrahamic Covenant. However, the Abrahamic Covenant was characterized by grace and faith while the Mosaic and Palestinian Covenants were characterized by law and works. These things together show the marvellous inter-relatedness of the covenants of creation and redemption.

Finally, the Everlasting Covenant, made in the heavens, in eternity past, between the Divine Persons, is revealed to be the all-inclusive covenant. It includes in itself the covenant of creation and all the covenants of redemption. As noted previously, all covenants made by God on the earth relative to mankind are but the progressive unfolding of this covenant of eternity. The New Covenant (the end) makes possible the Edenic Covenant (the beginning) and all other covenants between are but links in the covenantal chain of Divine revelation.

Chapter 2

THE EDENIC COVENANT

The Edenic Covenant is the Covenant God made with Adam and Eve in the Garden of Eden before the entrance of sin expressing His purpose in Creation. Genesis 1:1; 2:25.

INTRODUCTION

Genesis 1 and 2 not only record the creation of the heaven and earth but also some of the reasons why God made them. The prophet Isaiah stated that when God created the heaven and earth He did not create it in vain but "He formed it to be inhabited" (Isaiah 45:18).

In Genesis 1:1-19 God, as the wise master-builder prepared "the house" of the heaven and earth. In Genesis 1:20-31 God created animals to live in "the house" and man to rule over them as the masterpiece of creation. Verses 26-31 indicate that man was the focal point of God's creation. All of God's purposes were to centre in him. Thus, the first covenant was given to the first man and woman to reveal God's purpose in creating them. This Edenic Covenant was the first expression on earth of the pre-existent Everlasting Covenant in heaven (refer to Chapter 10 "The Everlasting Covenant"). The fact that man was the recipient but not the originator of the first covenant illustrates God's desire and purpose that man be in covenantal relationship with Himself. There could be no relationship with God apart from covenant. Thus while God was creating man, He was also declaring His covenant purposes over man (Genesis 1:26,27). Man, made in the image of God as a free-will creation, was placed on a period of probation to test his voluntary commitment to the covenant.

NOTE: Though the word "covenant" is not used until Genesis 6:18, there is enough covenantal language and covenantal elements in Genesis 1 and 2 as well as subsequent Scriptural support to confirm the integrity of the Edenic Covenant (See Jeremiah 31:35-37; 33:19-25; Genesis 8:22 with Genesis 1:14-19 and Psalms 89:34-37).

I.   **The WORDS of the Covenant**

    A.   **The Promises of the Covenant**

        The promises of the Edenic Covenant are expressions of God's purposes in creating man. Thus they are worded more as statements of purpose and command than as statements of promise.

        1.   **Promises of Blessing** (Genesis 1:28)

            a.   **Made in God's image, after His likeness** (Genesis 1:26,27)

                This image was spiritual, mental and volitional. It involved the very character and nature of God (Romans 8:28,29; Hebrews 1:3; I Corinthians 15:45-49; II Corinthians 3:18; 4:1; Colossians 3:10).

b. **Fruitfulness and multiplicity** (Genesis 1:28)

This fruitfulness involved both natural and spiritual reproduction. It involved populating the earth with a race of beings that would know God, be like Him and serve Him. Adam and Eve were to reproduce after their kind (Genesis 1:11,12; 5:1-3; John 15:16; Acts 6:1; 9:31; Philemon 10).

c. **To subdue the earth** (Genesis 1:28)

This subduing denotes warfare in that it means "to tread down, to conquer and to subjugate". This implied the existence of an enemy that Adam was to conquer. Adam was to conquer Satan, the only enemy then in existence, as well as to make the whole earth as the Garden of Eden (Joshua 18:1; Numbers 32:22,29; Ezekiel 36:34,35; Romans 16:20; I John 2:13,14; Revelation 3:21).

d. **To have dominion** (Genesis 1:28)

This dominion involved rulership over the earthly creation and would also include spiritual authority. Adam would be king under God (Genesis 2:19,20; Psalms 8:3-9; Revelation 1:6; 5:9,10; Luke 10:19; Hebrews 2:5-8).

e. **To eat herbs and fruit** (Genesis 1:29)

This involved the sustenance for man's physical existence (Genesis 2:9; Matthew 11:19; John 4:32-34). Eating meats was not allowed until the Noahic Covenant.

f. **To till the ground** (Genesis 2:5,15)

This involved man's occupation. He was created to work (II Thessalonians 3:6-12; Proverbs 24:30-34; John 9:4; 14:12).

2. **Promises of Cursing** (Genesis 2:17)

God promised Adam that if he disobeyed God's command and partook of the forbidden fruit, he would suffer the curse of death. This involved both spiritual and physical death (Deuteronomy 30:19; Romans 6:23; 5:12-21; I Corinthians 15:21,22).

B. **The Terms of the Covenant**

The blessings of the covenant were made available to man on the basis of the term of trusting obedience or, faith and obedience. Adam was given only one commandment of prohibition. He was forbidden to partake of the fruit of the tree of knowledge of good and evil (Genesis 2:9,16,17; Romans 5:12-21; Revelation 22:14; Deuteronomy 11:26-28).

C. **The Oath of the Covenant**

There is no Biblical record of an oath being attached to the Edenic Covenant.

D. **The Book of the Covenant**

Although no book was written at that time, this covenant was later recorded in the Book of Genesis.

II. **The BLOOD of the Covenant**

    A. **The Sacrifice of the Covenant**

The preparation for the fulfilment of the covenant involved Adam giving of his own life. His sacrificial giving involved his laying down in a deep sleep, the opening of his side, the giving of his body from which God built a bride. This may have also involved the shedding of sinless blood. Adam's recognition of this sacrifice is found in the statement that his bride was "bone of his bone and flesh of his flesh" (Genesis 2:18-25). The first bride and bridegroom of creation typified the bride and bridegroom of redemption, Christ and His Church (Ephesians 5:23-33).

    B. **The Mediator of the Covenant**

It is evident from Genesis 2:21,22 that God Himself acted as the mediator of this covenant. He put Adam to sleep, opened Adam's side and prepared his bride. Genesis 1:26,27, in using the Hebrew uni-plural title for God, Elohim, implies the involvement of the Godhead as the covenantors, even the Father, Son and Holy Spirit. In this passage both a plural image ("our image"), and a singular image ("his image") are referred to. Subsequent Scripture substantiates that Christ is the express image of God as well as the mediatorial person of the Godhead (Hebrews 1:3; Colossians 1:15; II Corinthians 4:4; Hebrews 8:6; 12:24; Galatians 3:20 Amplified; Romans 5:14).

    C. **The Sanctuary of the Covenant**

The place where the covenant was given, the sacrifice made and the mediatorial work of the covenantors performed was the Garden of Eden, the earthly Paradise. This was the place where God's presence appeared on earth fellow-shipping with man in the cool of the evening. This was God's earthly sanctuary containing the tree of life. This truth is confirmed by later Scriptures which reveal that the heavenly Paradise (the eternal dwelling place of God) contains the tree of eternal life (Genesis 3:24; II Corinthians 12:3-5; Revelation 2:7; 22:14).

III. **The SEAL of the Covenant**

The visible sign or token of the covenant was the tree of life. Of all the trees in the garden, only two were named and were placed "in the midst" of it. Of these two Adam was allowed to partake of only one, the tree of life. When he broke the terms of the covenant, God's judgment focused on withholding this tree from Adam. These facts indicate the tree of life to be the unique, tangible sign of the Edenic Covenant.

The final witness to man's full redemption and being restored to full covenantal relationship is his being given freedom of access to the tree of life which is in the Paradise of God (Genesis 2:17; 3:22-24; John 5:56-58; Revelation 2:7; 22:14).

SUMMARY

This covenant stands unique as it is the only covenant made with man before the entrance of sin. It declared God's creative purpose for man including covenantal relationship, character, dominion, fruitfulness and eternal life upon obedience and faith. The fall of man necessitated the revelation of the redemptive covenants to bring this covenant to fulfilment. This was particularly made possible by the New Covenant, which restores to man all that was lost in the Edenic Covenant.

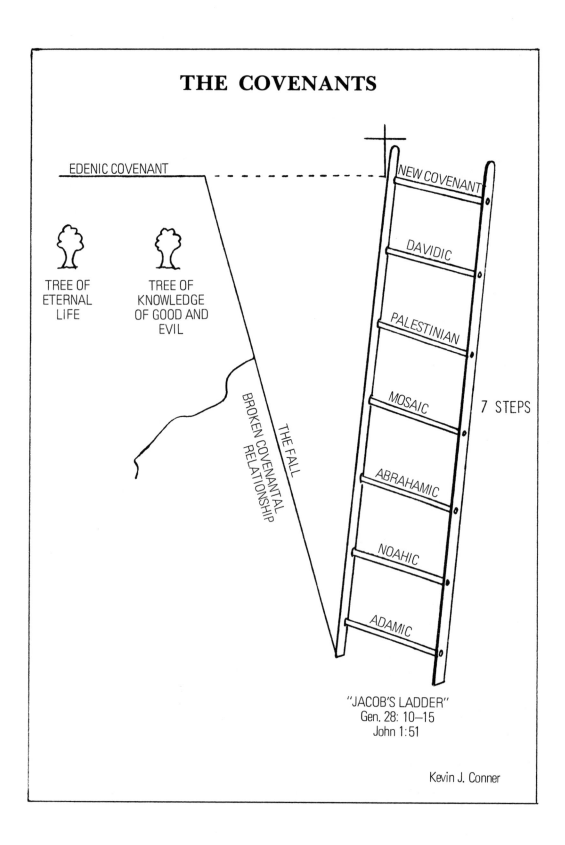

Chapter 3

THE ADAMIC COVENANT

> The Adamic Covenant is the Covenant God made with Adam and Eve in the Garden of Eden after the entrance of sin expressing His purpose in redemption. Genesis 3.

INTRODUCTION

Under the Edenic Covenant man was put on probation to test his commitment to the terms of the covenant. The one prohibition to not eat of the tree of knowledge of good and evil constituted the test of faith and obedience (Genesis 2:16,17). The test was occasioned by God's permitting the serpent's entrance into the Garden. The temptation to break the covenant came from Satan as he attacked the terms of the covenant. His aim was to break the covenantal relationship between the Creator and the creature by deceiving man into violating the covenant. He knew this would rob man of the blessings and put him under the curses of the covenant. Satan's attack was upon the covenantal God and the covenantal man, but his approach was to attack the covenantal language. Genesis 3:1-6 records the serpent's tempting of the woman and their progressive undermining of the words of the covenant.

1. The serpent *questions* the Word, "Hath God said . . ." Vs1.

2. The woman *adds* to the Word, ". . . neither shall ye touch it." Vs3.

3. The woman *weakens* the Word, "lest ye die." Vs3 (Genesis 2:17).
    Note — Deuteronomy 4:2; Proverbs 30:6; Revelation 22:18-19.

4. The serpent *lies* against the Word, "You will not surely die." Vs4.

5. The serpent *misinterprets* the Word, "You shall be as gods." Vs5 (II Corinthians 4:2)

At this point, being deceived by the serpent, the woman partook of the forbidden fruit and gave to Adam also. This unbelief and disobedience broke their covenantal relationship and brought them under the curse of the covenant (Genesis 3:6,7; I Timothy 2:13-15; Romans 5:12-21; 14:23; Hosea 6:7; I John 3:4).

The results of the fall of man were that man's *covenantal relationship was broken, his character* was corrupted by the entrance of sin, his *dominion* was lost and he and his *offspring* came under the dominion of sin and death (I Corinthians 15:45-49; Romans 5:12).

This set the stage for the revelation of the Adamic Covenant. God came in grace to fallen man seeking to restore him back to covenantal relationship. This Adamic Covenant was the beginning of the covenants of redemption. Upon the foundation of the Edenic Covenant the Adamic Covenant constitutes the most comprehensive prophecy that God ever gave to mankind, in that it encompasses all successive covenants of redemption. It is a "seed" covenant to the others which follow.

I.   **The WORDS of the Covenant**

    A.   **The Promises of the Covenant**

The promises of the Adamic Covenant are expressions of God's purposes in redeeming man and judging Satan.

    1.   **Promises of Blessing** (Genesis 3:15)

The seed of the woman would bruise the serpent's head. This seed would crush, conquer and subjugate Satan and all the realm of his authority. This promise involved the chosen seed of Israel, the virgin birth of Christ, His ministry, the Church and the eternal judgment of Satan and his kingdom (Joshua 10:24; Psalms 60:12; Luke 10:19; Romans 16:20). This seed promise is progressively unfolded in the succeeding covenants and consummates in Christ and the Church.

    2.   **Promises of Cursing** (Genesis 3:14-19)

While the curse of God came on the serpent and the earth, God did not curse the man and the woman made in His own image. However, the man and woman were affected by the curse and come under Divine judgment.

        a.   **Curse on the Serpent** (Genesis 3:14)

The natural serpent which was used as a tool of Satan is irrevocably humiliated to the dust of the earth. The serpent has ever since borne the stigma of its association with Satan (Revelation 12:9).

        b.   **Curse on the Devil** (Genesis 3:14)

The curse extended beyond the natural serpent to the Devil himself who is "that old serpent" (Revelation 12:9; 20:1-3). An irrevocable curse was put upon him leading up to his ultimate crushing (Romans 16:20; Revelation 12; 20:10).

        c.   **Judgment on the Woman** (Genesis 3:16)

The judgment on the woman involved multiplied conception, sorrow in child-birth and subservience to her husband (I Timothy 2:13-15; I Corinthians 11:7-9).

        d.   **Judgment on the Man** (Genesis 3:17,19)

The judgment on the man involved sweat, toil and sorrow in labouring with a cursed earth until his death.

        e.   **Curse on the Earth** (Genesis 3:17,18)

The soil of the earth was cursed to bring forth thorns and thistles. Instead of readily bringing forth food for man, it would of its own accord hinder man's efforts for food.

        f.   **Curse on the Animal Kingdom**

Romans 8:20-22 indicates that the creatures of the earth were affected by the fall of man and became wild and carnivorous (Contrast this with Genesis 2:19,20).

        g.   **Judgment of Sin by Death** (Genesis 2:17; 3:19)

As stated under the Edenic Covenant God confirmed under the

Adamic Covenant that the wages of sin is death. This involved physical, spiritual and eternal death (Romans 6:23; Ezekiel 18:19; Ephesians 2:1,5; I Timothy 5:6; Revelation 14:11; 20:11-15).

h. **Judgment by Expulsion from Eden** (Genesis 3:23,24)

The final act of judgment upon the man and the woman was to expel them from the Paradise that God had placed them in. This was to keep them from partaking of the tree of life and living forever in an un-redeemable state (Revelation 2:7; 22:14).

B. **Terms of the Covenant**

In that man had fallen from the obedience of the Edenic Covenant, the covenant of creation, God sought to restore man back to that obedience through the Adamic Covenant, the covenant of redemption. Adam's dis-obedience was the result of his unbelief. Thus the emphasis of the terms of the Adamic Covenant (as in all covenants) was upon faith and trust in God (Hebrews 11:6; Romans 14:23; John 16:8). The evidence of Adam and Eve's faith is seen in:

1. Adam's naming Eve as "the mother of all living" (Genesis 3:15,16,20).

2. Adam and Eve receiving the coats of skin in exchange for their self-made covering of fig leaves (Genesis 3:21).

3. Eve's faith-response at the birth of Cain (Genesis 3:15; 4:1).

4. Adam's communication of faith-sacrifices to his children (Genesis 4:1-4; Hebrews 11:4; I John 3:12).

C. **The Oath of the Covenant**

There is no Biblical record of an oath being attached to the Adamic Covenant.

D. **The Book of the Covenant**

Although no book was written at this time, this covenant was later recorded in the Book of Genesis by Moses under the inspiration of the Spirit of God.

II. **The BLOOD of the Covenant**

A. **The Sacrifice of the Covenant**

After Adam and Eve fell from covenantal relationship and their conscience was awakened and smitten with guilt, they sought to cover their own sin and make themselves acceptable to God and to each other. The law of conscience led to the law of works (Romans 5:12-14; 3:27). The man-made fig-leaf coverings were an attempt to make themselves righteous and acceptable before God. However, God judged self-righteousness to be insufficient (Isaiah 64:6). It was up to God to move in grace to deal with man's sin and provide an acceptable covering. In that man had broken the life commitment of the Edenic Covenant, and was deserving of death, death had to take place in order for his sin to be covered. God introduced a substitutionary sacrificial death in order to cover man's sinfulness. This is implied in Genesis 3:21 when God clothed them with coats of skin, which had to have come from a slain innocent animal. Thus, based on substitutionary body and blood Adam and Eve were clothed in the death of another. The innocent died for the guilty, and the sinless animal was sacrificed for sinful man. This covenant sacrifice was the first of all animal sacrifices that pointed to the New Covenant sacrifice, the body and blood the Lord Jesus Christ (John 1:29,36; Hebrews 10:1-12).

B. **The Mediator of the Covenant**

1. **The Priesthood of Christ**

    It is evident from Genesis 3:21 that God Himself acted as the mediator of this covenant. He slew the animals, He made the coats of skin and He clothed Adam and Eve with them. Although the creatorship name of Elohim (God) was used in relation to the Edenic Covenant of creation before the entrance of sin, it is the redemptive name of Jehovah (Lord) that is used in relation to the Adamic Covenant of redemption after the entrance of sin. The name attached to this covenant is "the LORD GOD" which embodied in itself both creation and redemption (Genesis 3:14, 21,22,23).

    Further Scripture reveals that the mediatorial person in the Godhead is the Lord Jesus Christ (Hebrews 9:15; I Timothy 2:5; Hebrews 12:24).

2. **The Priesthood of Adam**

    This scene also initiated the development of the patriarchal priesthood. As the Lord God demonstrated His own priesthood on Adam's behalf He set an example for Adam to follow in being the priest of his own household. This was later substantiated in that the Levitical Priesthood, under the Mosaic Covenant, were given the coats of skin of certain animal sacrifices (Leviticus 7:8). It was also illustrated in Job's priesthood for his own family (Job 1:1-5).

C. **The Sanctuary of the Covenant**

The place where the covenant was given, the sacrifice made and the mediatorial work of the covenantors fulfilled was the Garden of Eden. However, the focus in Genesis 3:21-24 seems to be on a place at the east of Eden's garden. The revelation of the sanctuary under the Mosaic Covenant confirms the sanctuary language of the Adamic Covenant.

1. God *placed* (Hebrew "caused to dwell") His presence (Genesis 3:24; 4:16 with Exodus 25:8).

2. This place was at the *east* (Genesis 3:24; with Leviticus 16:14; Ezekiel 43:1-4).

3. The *Cherubims* were placed there as guardians (Genesis 3:24 with Exodus 25:17-22).

4. A *flaming sword* was placed there also to keep the way to the tree of life (Genesis 3:24; Exodus 26:33).

5. This is the most suitable place for Cain and Abel to have brought their *offerings* unto the Lord (Genesis 4:1-4; Hebrews 12:4).

III. **The SEAL of the Covenant**

Having forfeited the seal of the Edenic Covenant, Adam and Eve received the coats of skin as tokens to them of their faith in the atoning sacrifice of the Adamic Covenant (Genesis 3:21). This pointed to the faith-righteousness that the Holy Spirit brings to the New Covenant believer who accepts the body and blood of the sacrifice of Jesus Christ (Isaiah 61:10; Romans 4:1-5).

SUMMARY

The Adamic Covenant is a "seed" covenant introducing the covenants of redemption. The covenantal language that is expressed in "seed" form in this covenant is developed in fulness in the covenants which follow, leading up to its ultimate fulfilment in the New Covenant. Jesus Christ as the seed of the woman fulfills this Covenant in redeeming man back to perfect and eternal covenantal relationship with God.

Chapter 4

THE NOAHIC COVENANT

The Noahic Covenant is the Covenant God made with Noah after the Flood involving all creatures and all future generations of mankind. It confirms and adds to God's purpose as stated in the Edenic Covenant.

INTRODUCTION

Under the Adamic Covenant man was put on probation to test his faith and obedience to the covenant. The importance of man's obedience to God, the necessity of conquering Satan, the place of diligence in work, and the trust in the substitutionary death of an animal for their faith-covering were emphasized in the Adamic Covenant. This put a requirement on man to live up to these realities. It was, once again, a period of probation extending from Adam to Noah. During this time, the human race became divided into two groups, those who believed and obeyed God and those who refused. Beginning with Cain and Abel two seed lines developed until the days of Noah; the ungodly (Genesis 4) and the godly (Genesis 5). Though man was under the law of conscience, the law of sin continued to drive him away from covenantal relationship with God. Cain's rejection of the covenant sacrifice and murder of his covenant brother, Abel, led eventually to the corruption of the entire human race with one exception; "Noah found grace in the eyes of the Lord" (Genesis 4:1-24; 6:1-13).

The days of Noah were characterized by intermarriage, great wickedness, evil imaginations and desires, corruption and violence. This total failure to keep the covenant demanded God's judgment (Genesis 6:1-13; Matthew 24:37-39). The judgment from breaking the Edenic Covenant was death and expulsion from Eden while the judgment for breaking the Adamic Covenant was death by a universal flood.

Even before the judgment was executed, God began to move in covenant grace to preserve His next covenant man. Out of the godly line God chose Noah, a man who was keeping the Adamic Covenant (Genesis 6:8,9; 7:1). He was told to build an ark of safety to preserve his household and certain of the animal kingdom. This he did in obedience to God's commandment (Gensis 6-7-8; Hebrews 11:7; I Peter 3:30; II Peter 2:5).

When Noah departed from the ark after the Flood, God made a covenant with him, his family and all creatures. This constituted a new beginning for man upon an earth cleansed from sinful flesh.

I.   **The WORDS of the Covenant**

   A.   **The Promises of the Covenant**

   The promises of the Noahic Covenant reinstate God's purpose for man as stated in the Edenic Covenant adding certain restrictions and responsibilities.

   1.   **Promises of Blessing** (Genesis 8:15-19,21,22; 9:1-7,11,15)

      a.   **God's Blessing upon Noah and his sons** (Genesis 9:1)

      God promised Noah that His favour and benevolence would remain on him and his family (Isaiah 54:9,10; Hebrews 11:7).

b. **Fruitfulness and Multiplicity** (Genesis 9:1,7; 8:15-17)

This fruitfulness involved both natural and spiritual reproduction. It involved re-populating the earth with people that would be in covenantal relationship with God (Genesis 1:18; John 15:16; Acts 9:31).

c. **Ruling over Creatures** (Genesis 9:2)

The creatures of the earth were made subject to man's authority, to be ruled by fear and dread (Genesis 2:19,20; Romans 8:20-22).

d. **Eating of Meats** (Genesis 9:3)

For the first time man was allowed to eat meat as well as herbs. Though "clean and unclean" animals were distinguished going into the ark none were forbidden to Noah to be eaten (Genesis 1:29,30; 2:9,16; 6:18-22; 7:1-3; I Timothy 4:1-5; Hebrews 13:9; Romans 14:1-6,14,15). Prohibition of unclean meats was not given until the Mosaic Covenant which was given to the nation of Israel (Leviticus 11).

e. **Earth Preserved from further Curse** (Genesis 8:21)

Though the ground was cursed under the Adamic Covenant, God promised that He would for man's sake restrain any further curse (Genesis 3:17-19; Revelation 22:3).

f. **Creatures preserved from annihilation** (Genesis 8:21)

Though the creatures would be ruled by fear and dread and affected by the results of sin, the animal creation would not be totally destroyed by God (Jonah 4:11; Psalm 104:9-29; Romans 8:19-23).

g. **Four Seasons established** (Genesis 8:22)

Under the Edenic Covenant, the sun, moon and stars were given for signs and seasons, days and years (Genesis 1:14-19). However, from Adam to Noah the earth had a constant climate and was watered by a mist rather than rain (Genesis 2:5-6; 7:4). Though the earth was cursed before the flood the seasons were established after the flood to further affect man's toil with the cursed earth. These seasons were to be a blessing to man upon his obedience to the covenant but could be turned into judgment upon his disobedience (Deuteronomy 11:10-17; Psalm 1:3; Acts 3:19-21; I Thessalonians 5:1,2; Ecclesiastes 3:1; Song of Solomon 2:11-13).

h. **No more Universal Flood** (Genesis 9:11,15)

To free man from the fear of another universal deluge God promised to never destroy the earth again with a flood. Though there have been many local floods the earth is never again to be destroyed by water (Isaiah 54:9,10; II Peter 3:5-7).

2. **Promises of Cursing** (Genesis 9:25-27)

The curse given in relation to this covenant is a part of the progressive unfolding of the curses in Scripture. Under the Adamic Covenant the curse was placed upon the serpent and the earth (Genesis 3:14-17; 8:21). The first man to be cursed was Cain who was a liar, murderer and blood-of-the-lamb rejector (Genesis 4:1-16). As the son of Adam came under a curse, so

Ham, a son of Noah, brought his son under a curse. When Ham dishonored his father in relation to his nakedness he brought a curse upon Canaan his son (Genesis 9:20-27; Leviticus 18:6,7).

3. **National and Temporal** (Genesis 9:25-27)

From the three sons of Noah the earth was repopulated and divided into families, tongues, lands and nations (Genesis 9:18,19; 10:5,20,31,32).

a. **Shem** (Genesis 9:26,27; 10:21-31; 11:10-32)

Shem was to be a blessed race having Canaan as his servant and being a blessing to Japheth. The Biblical history of the nation of Israel illustrates this.

b. **Ham** (Genesis 9:24-27; 10:6-20)

As Noah was affected by the sin of his son, Ham, so Ham as a father was judged in his son, Canaan. Canaan was cursed and was to be a servant of servants to both Shem and Japheth. The Biblical history of the Canaanite nations illustrates this.

c. **Japheth** (Genesis 9:27; 10:2-5)

Japheth was to be blessed with enlargement. He was to dwell in the tents of Shem, and Canaan was also to be his servant. Subsequent history illustrates that the Japhetic races were given large parts of the earth to dwell in and were blessed therein.

4. **Spiritual and Eternal** (Genesis 9:25-27)

Shem was blessed by God for honoring his father and was chosen to be the progenitor of the godly seed line. From him came Abraham, Isaac, Jacob, Moses, Israel, David and the Messiah who were all given covenants of redemption (Romans 9:4-6; Luke 3:23-38). It was to be through the seed of Shem that the Messianic blessing would come on all families of the earth.

B. **The Terms of the Covenant**

1. **Faith and Obedience**

Noah was a man who believed and obeyed the commandments of the Lord (Genesis 6:22; 7:5; Hebrews 11:7; I Peter 3:20; II Peter 2:5).

2. **Not to eat blood** (Genesis 9:4)

Though man was permitted to eat meats under this covenant, he was not to eat blood. God stated that the blood represents life and the shedding of blood represents death. Because God established the shedding of animal blood as the substitutionary sacrifice for man's sin, He has reserved the blood unto Himself and thus forbade man to partake of it. The Mosaic Covenant later confirmed this restriction, which was to ensure that man would neither believe that the sacrifice of the animal could cleanse him from sin, nor that he could receive the life of the animal (Leviticus 3:17; 17:10-16; Deuteronomy 12:16). Life and cleansing would in due time come through the incorruptible blood of the Lamb of God, the Lord Jesus Christ (John 6:55-63).

3. Murder Forbidden (Genesis 9:5,6)

In response to the violence beginning with Cain and increasing to the days of Noah, God specifically forbade murder. This was to remind man of how valuable the life of man made in the image of God was. This protection of human life was confirmed and amplified under the Mosaic Covenant (Exodus 20:13; Numbers 35).

4. **Capital Punishment** (Genesis 9:5,6)

With the prohibition of murder came the punishment for it. Under the Adamic Covenant murderers were judged by God Himself, as with Cain and Abel (Genesis 4). With the Noahic Covenant God delegated the authority to man to deal with murderers. The death penalty as the highest act of governmental authority implies all lesser levels of human government. The Mosaic Covenant confirmed the principles of a "life for a life" whether by man or beast (Exodus 21:23-25; Leviticus 24:17-22; Deuteronomy 19:21; Numbers 35). Under the New Covenant, the institution of human government is fully endorsed even to the extent of capital punishment (Matthew 22:17-21; I Timothy 2:1-4; I Peter 2:17). Paul's reference to the sword of the state would have clearly indicated to the Church at Rome the right of execution (Romans 13:1-7). Though murderers may escape capital punishment in this life there is eternal punishment for unrepentant murderers (Revelation 21:8; 22:15).

C. **The OATH of the Covenant**

Though the word "oath" is not specifically used in Genesis 8 and 9, Isaiah 54:9 reveals that God did attach His oath to the Noahic Covenant. This confirmation of God's commitment to the covenant promises made it irrevocable (Hebrews 6:13-20).

D. **The Book**

Though there is no specific account of this covenant being written in a book, it does find its place, as do previous covenants, in the Book of Genesis.

II. **The BLOOD of the Covenant**

A. **The Sacrifice of the Covenant**

Though Noah took both clean and unclean animals into the ark, only clean animals were sacrificed to God as burnt offerings. This animal body and blood constituted the sacrifice of the Noahic Covenant and was a "sweet savour" unto the Lord (Genesis 6:19,20; 7:2,3,8,9; 8:20).

Under the Mosaic Covenant voluntary offerings were "sweet savour" offerings, while compulsory offerings were "non-sweet" sacrifices (Leviticus 1-7).

B. **The Mediator of the Covenant**

Following the pattern of the Adamic Covenant Noah functioned as the patriarchal king-priest of his house. The fact of his offering the sacrifice unto God demonstrated his priestly office (Genesis 8:20; Hebrews 8:3). Adam, Noah, Job and Abraham all illustrate the existence of the household priesthood order. The fullest illustration of the details of priestly ministry came later under the Mosaic Covenant. Noah's priesthood pointed to the ultimate mediator who began a new creation — Jesus Christ.

C.   **The Sanctuary of the Covenant**

Noah's altar is the first mention of an altar in Scripture (Genesis 8:20). In that this was the place where the priest offered his sacrifice, the altar constituted the sanctuary of the patriarchs. Wherever God's covenant people built an altar, whether of earth or stone, there God promised to record His name, come to them, meet with them and bless them. This revelation of His presence would consecrate that place as being sacred and holy to the Lord (Exodus 20:24-26).

III.   **The SEAL of the Covenant**

Genesis 9:12-17 plainly states that the rainbow was given by God as the token of the Noahic Covenant. God placed a sign in the sky between heaven and earth, and between God and man. God committed Himself to look upon it as He looked towards earth and remember His covenant mercy. Likewise man was to look upon it as he looked toward heaven and remember with faith God's covenant promise. In that this covenant was made with the whole earth for the duration of its existence, all the world may witness to the fact that God is a covenant keeping God.

Subsequent Scripture reveals that the rainbow is also around God's throne, indicating that all the administrations of God's authority in relation to earth and to man pass through the remembrance of His covenant mercy (Ezekiel 1:28; Revelation 4:3). The ultimate revelation of the token of the Noahic Covenant is seen in the Lord Jesus Christ, the mediator of the New Covenant, having the rainbow around His head (Revelation 10:1).

SUMMARY

The Noahic Covenant contains a reaffirmation of the creative purposes of God as stated in the Edenic Covenant. It is also an extension of "the seed" promises of redemption as in the Adamic Covenant. Though it arises out of a time of great judgment, it establishes a hope that God's purposes in creation will be fulfilled through redemption. The hope of the Noahic Covenant finds its complete fulfilment in the New Covenant.

Chapter 5

THE ABRAHAMIC COVENANT

> The Abrahamic Covenant is the Covenant God made with Abraham, Isaac and Jacob. It was made after the tower of Babel and the scattering of the descendants of Noah. It involves National Israel, the Seed Messiah, and all believers of all nations. It is the most comprehensive of all Old Testament Covenants.

INTRODUCTION

As seen in connection with the previous covenants, each covenant begins a probation cycle.

1.   Man's *probation* in relation to the terms of the covenant given.

2.   Man's *failure* to keep the terms.

3.   God's *judgment* on sin.

4.   God's *redemptive* covenant given.

With the establishment of the Noahic Covenant and the new beginning on a cleansed earth came a further period of probation. There were further terms added to those of the previous covenants, as God continued to unfold His ways to man.

Soon after the giving of the Noahic Covenant, the failure of man began to evidence itself. Noah's drunkenness and nakedness and Ham's disrespect to his father were failures in relation to God's reproductive purposes for man as stated in the Noahic Covenant (Genesis 9:1). Their conduct was not consistent with the high and holy purpose God intended for the powers of reproduction. This failure in the family of Noah led to the failure of the entire race at the Tower of Babel. Nimrod, of the line of Ham, led a rebellion against God's command to replenish the earth by drawing the people together at Babel. This rebellion was epitomized in the building of the Tower of Babel to reach unto heaven to the glory of man and the defiance of God (Genesis 10:6-10; 11:1-4). They took the delegated authority of human government given in the Noahic Covenant and turned it against God and His government. Thus, human government was usurping the place of Divine government.

God foresaw that man's unified rebellion would soon deserve universal judgment. Thus, in judgment with a view to mercy, God stepped into the scene at Babel and brought man's evil unity into confusion. By confusing their languages, scattering them across the earth and dividing them into nations, God was setting the stage for the unfolding of His redemptive purpose among the nations (Genesis 10:25,31,32; 11:5-9; Acts 17:26,27; Deuteronomy 32:8).

While the families were developing into nations in their respective places God chose the next covenant man from the line of Shem. It would be through Abram that God would bless all the nations of the earth (Genesis 11:10-32; 12:1-3).

I.   **The WORDS of the Covenant**

A.   **The Promises of the Covenant**

The promises of the Abrahamic Covenant comprehend the promises of the previous and also subsequent covenants. The Abrahamic Covenant enlarges upon the Edenic, Adamic and Noahic Covenants. It also includes in itself the covenants relative to the chosen nation of Israel, which are the Mosaic, Palestinian, Davidic and New Covenants (Romans 9:4-5).

This covenant was not only made with Abraham, but its oath was given to Isaac and it was confirmed to Jacob and then Israel after him (I Chronicles 16:15-17). These three fathers were together partakers of one covenant; even as the three persons in the eternal Godhead are partakers of one covenant (Exodus 2:24; 3:6,15).

The covenant as given to the three fathers and to Israel is stated in the following major passages:

*   **To Abraham**

    Genesis 12:1-3; 13:14-18; 15:1-21; 17:1-27; 18:17-19; 21:12; 22:1-18.

*   **To Isaac**

    Genesis 24:60; 26:1-5,24.

*   **To Jacob**

    Genesis 27:28-29; 28:1-4,13-22; 32:12,28; 35:10-12; 48:3-4.

*   **To Israel**

    Deuteronomy 7:6-16; I Chronicles 16:15-22; Psalm 105:8-15; Micah 7:20; Exodus 3:15; 32:13; Hebrews 6:13-14.

1.   **Promises of Blessing**

a.   **Personal Blessing** (Genesis 12:2)

God said to Abraham "I will bless thee" indicating God's desire to bestow His favour upon Abraham himself. This promise was confirmed to Isaac (Genesis 26:3), Jacob (Genesis 28:3) and to Israel (Deuteronomy 28:1-8).

This was fulfilled in:

*   The blessing of Melchisedek in the bread and the wine given to him (Genesis 14:19-20).

*   The blessing of material prosperity (Genesis 13:2; 24:1,35).

*   The blessing of physical well-being (Romans 4:17-21).

This blessing was also fulfilled in the lives of Isaac (Genesis 26:12-14), Jacob (Genesis 30) and in Israel (Deuteronomy 8:18).

b.   **Blessing Others** (Genesis 12:2)

God also said to Abraham "Thou shalt be a blessing." God made it clear to Abraham that the purpose of being blessed was that he might be a blessing to others. This promise was confirmed to Isaac, Jacob and to Israel.

This was fulfilled in:

* The blessing of Abraham's own household (Genesis 14:14; 18:19; 24:35).

* The blessing of Abraham's benevolence to Lot in allowing his choice of the land and also in his rescue from Sodom's destruction (Genesis 13:5-9; 14:1-16; 18:16-33).

* The blessing of healing of the Gentile Abimelech's household (Genesis 20:17).

* The blessing of covenantal relationship with a Gentile, King Abimelech of the Philistines (Genesis 21:22-32).

We find the same promises of blessing fulfilled in the lives of Isaac and Jacob (Genesis 30:37) as well as the nation of Israel (Deuteronomy 28:1-14).

c. **Blessed by Others** (Genesis 12:3)

God also said to Abraham "I will bless them that bless thee." As a confirmation of His blessing, God promised to bless those who show favor to Abraham. This promise was confirmed also to Isaac (Genesis 26:12-33), Jacob (Genesis 30:25-43) and Israel (Numbers 24:9).

This was fulfilled in:

* The blessing of Rebekah's family for responding to the request of Abraham for a bride for his son, Isaac (Genesis 24:51-53).

* This was also fulfilled in Isaac (Genesis 26), Jacob (Genesis 29,30,31) and the nation of Israel (Deuteronomy 27-28).

d. **Messianic Blessing** (Genesis 12:3; 22:17-18)

God also promised Abraham "in thee shall all families of the earth be blessed." This was the greatest promise of blessing, that through Abraham God would bestow His favor upon all the peoples of the earth. This promise involved the birth of the Seed Messiah, Jesus Christ, and was fulfilled in the New Covenant.

It was confirmed to Isaac (Genesis 26:4), to Jacob (Genesis 28:14), to Judah (Genesis 49:8-12), to Israel (Numbers 24:17) and finally to David (II Samuel 7; Psalms 89,132).

This was fulfilled in:

* The blessing of the Gospel of Christ, who is the seed of Abraham, Isaac and Jacob, as well as of Judah through David (Galatians 3:8,16,29; Matthew 1:1; Romans 1:3; 16:20; Genesis 3:15).

e. **Blessing of a Great Name** (Genesis 12:2)

God further promised "Abraham that He would "make thy name great." Abraham was to be given an honorable and well-known name.

This was fulfilled in:

* The blessing of the new name of Abraham given at the time of circumcision (Genesis 17:5; Acts 7:8).

* The blessing of a good reputation (Genesis 24:35).

* The blessing of association with God; "The God of Abraham, the God of Isaac, and the God of Jacob" (Genesis 24:12; 26:24; 28:13; Exodus 3:15; Mark 12:26-27).

* The blessing of many nations who would revere his name (John 8). There are three major religious groupings that honor the name of Abraham; Islam, Judaism and Christianity.

* The blessing of a name of faith as "the father of all who believe" (Romans 4:11-16).

f. **Blessing of Multiplicity of Seed**

The blessing of multiplicity of seed was through the years given progressively to Abraham, Sarah, Isaac, Rebekah, Jacob and to Joseph's two sons, Ephraim and Manasseh.

(1) **To Abraham**

    (a) A great nation (Genesis 12:2).

    (b) Seed to be as the dust of the earth (Genesis 13:16).

    (c) Seed as the stars of heaven (Genesis 15:5).

    (d) To be a father of many nations (Genesis 17:4,5,6,7,8).

    (e) Seed to be as innumerable as the stars and the sand (Genesis 22:17-18).

(2) **To Sarah**

To be a mother of nations (Genesis 17:16).

(3) **To Rebekah**

To be the mother of thousands of millions (Genesis 24:60).

(4) **To Isaac**

Seed to be as the stars of heaven (Genesis 26:4).

(5) **To Jacob**

    (a) Seed to be as the dust of the earth (Genesis 28:14).

    (b) Seed to be as innumerable as the sand of the sea (Genesis 32:12).

    (c) A nation and company of nations to come of him (Genesis 35:11).

(6) **To Joseph**

Fruitfulness and a multitude of people (Genesis 48:4).

(7) **To Ephraim and Manasseh**

    (a) Ephraim and Manasseh would grow together as a multitude in the earth (Genesis 48:16).

    (b) Ephraim would become a multitude of nations (Genesis 48:19).

Together Ephraim and Manasseh would become a nation and a company of nations.

(8) **To Israel**

    (a) Israel was to be a holy nation (Exodus 19:6).

    (b) Israel was to be multiplied because of God's covenant (Leviticus 26:9).

    (c) Israel was to multiply and be blessed above all people in relation to the fruit of the womb (Deuteronomy 7:12-14).

    (d) Israel was to be as numberless as the sands of the seashore (Hosea 2:10).

All these promises of multiplicity of seed, a nation, nations and a multitude of nations find fulfillment in the following:

* The nations which come from Abraham through Hagar and Ishmael; that is predominantly the Arab nations (Genesis 21:13,18; 25:12-18).

* The nations which come from Abraham through Sarah and Isaac; that is in Bible times and history the united kingdom and nation of Israel, and then after the division of the nation the two nations of the House of Israel and the House of Judah (Ezekiel 37:15-28).

* The nations which come from Abraham's sons through Keturah and his concubines after Sarah's death; that is other nations including some Arab nations which trace themselves back to Abraham (Genesis 25:1-4, 6).

* The holy nation, the Church, made up of believers out of every kindred, tongue, tribe and nation (I Peter 2:5-10; Revelation 5:9-10; Ephesians 2:12-21).

* The Church is the true and spiritual Israel of God (Galatians 6:15-16; Romans 9:6-8). The believing Gentiles and believing Israelites are grafted into the olive tree and all together become one in "the commonwealth of Israel" (Romans 11; Ephesians 2:12). In Christ there is neither Jew nor Gentile but all believers are now the seed of Abraham (Galatians 3:28-29). Together they constitute the one new man and the body of Christ (Ephesians 3:1-9).

g. **Blessing of Land**

God promised Abraham that his seed would also have a land to dwell in. For Abraham to be the father of many nations there would have to be lands for that seed to dwell in. God set the bounds of the other nations according to the number of the children of Israel (Deuteronomy 32:8,9; Acts 17:26).

(1) **To Abraham**

    (a) God promised to show him a land (Genesis 12:1).

(b) God would give him and his seed the land forever (Genesis 13:14-18).

(c) The land would extend from the Euphrates river to Egypt (Genesis 15:7-21).

(d) All the land of Canaan would be an everlasting possession (Genesis 17:7,8).

(2) To Isaac

God promised that He would give "all these countries" to his seed (Genesis 26:2-4).

(3) To Jacob

(a) His seed would spread abroad to the north, south, east and west (Genesis 28:13-15).

(b) Land was promised for the nation and company of nations (Genesis 36:11,12).

(c) Canaan land was given to his seed for an everlasting possession (Genesis 48:3,4).

These land promises find their fulfillment in Israel conquering Canaan (Joshua through to David; Joshua 1-24; I Kings 4:20-25; II Chronicles 9:26), in other lands for the seed of Abraham (Genesis 36:8,9,43; II Samuel 7: 10-16), and also in Abraham being "heir of the world" (Romans 4:13). The ultimate fulfillment is in the heavenly country of which Canaan was an earthly shadow (Hebrews 11:8-16). As with all the promises of the Abrahamic Covenant there is both natural and spiritual fulfillment of the land promises.

NOTE:

The Palestinian Covenant was placed alongside of the Abrahamic Covenant adding conditions for maintaining possession of the land.

h. Blessing of Victory over Enemies

God promised Abraham that he would "possess the gate of his enemies" (Genesis 22:17). This promise of conquest of enemies was confirmed to Rebekah (Genesis 24:60) and to Judah (Genesis 49:8-12).

This was fulfilled in:

* Joshua's conquest of Canaan's 33 kings (Joshua 11,12).

* Judah's leadership in further victory in the land (Judges 1).

* David's victories over all his enemies (II Samuel 8; I Chronicles 22:8).

* The spiritual fulfillment in the Church's victory over the gates of hell (Matthew 16:18).

i. **Blessing of Kings**

God promised that Abraham would have descendants that would reign as kings (Genesis 17:6). It was confirmed to Sarah (Genesis 17:16), to Jacob (Genesis 35:11), to Judah (Genesis 49:8-12), to Israel (Deuteronomy 17:14-20; Numbers 23:21), and finally to David (II Samuel 7).

This was fulfilled in:

* The natural seed of Abraham (i.e., The Kings of Esau/Edom. Genesis 36).

* The chosen natural seed of Abraham (i.e., The Kings of Judah and Israel. II Chronicles 12:18,19; 14:15-18).

* Jesus Christ, the King of kings and Lord of lords (Revelation 19:16).

* The spiritual seed of Abraham, the Church (Revelation 1:6; 5:9-10).

NOTE:

The Davidic covenant was given later to confirm and fulfill this Abrahamic Covenant promise.

j. **Blessing of Divine Relationship**

God promised Abraham that He would be a God unto him and to his seed after him (Genesis 17:7,8). This was confirmed to Moses (Exodus 6:1-8) and the Prophets (Jeremiah 24:7; 30:22; 31:31-34; 32:38-40; Ezekiel 11:19,20; 36:25-28).

This was fulfilled in:

* Old Testament saints who knew God (i.e., Joseph, Joshua, Samuel, David, etc.).

* New Testament saints who know God through Christ (Hebrews 8:6-13; Revelation 21:3).

NOTE:

Though this relationship was broken under the Mosaic Covenant, it is restored through Christ under the New Covenant (Hosea 1:6-11 with I Peter 2:9-10; Romans 9:25-29).

2. Promises of Cursing

In that the Abrahamic Covenant is distinctly a covenant of blessing, the only curse attached to this covenant is actually a blessing for Abraham and his seed. God said to Abraham: "I will curse him that curseth thee" (Genesis 12:3). It was also confirmed to Isaac (Genesis 27:26-29). Even Balaam recognized that he could not curse the people God had blessed (Numbers 22:6; 23:8; 24:9).

B. The Terms of the Covenant

1. Faith

Both Old and New Testaments clearly show that Abraham's response to the promises of the covenant was one of faith. For this reason he has been called "the father of all who believe." Romans 4:3 states that "Abraham believed God and it was counted unto him for righteousness" (Genesis 15:6; Psalms 106:31; Galatians 3:6; Hebrews 11:8-19). His faith was tested and perfected as he progressed from "faith to faith" (Romans 1:17).

2. Obedience

Abraham's faith was proven by his unquestioning obedience and his obedience was sustained by his attitude of faith (Genesis 22:18; 26:5; Hebrews 11:8; James 2:20-24).

C. The Oath of the Covenant

The Abrahamic Covenant was one of the few covenants having an oath attached to it to make its promises irrevocable. The first statement of oath is given in connection with the typical death and resurrection of Isaac, the only begotten son of the Old Testament (Genesis 22:16-18; Hebrews 11:17-19). It was confirmed to Isaac (Genesis 26:2-5), and in subsequent Scriptures to Jacob and Israel (I Chronicles 16:16; Psalms 105:8-10; Deuteronomy 7:8; 29:9-13; Jeremiah 11:5; Micah 7:20; Acts 7:17; Luke 1:72,73). Hebrews 6:13-18 explains that when God made promise to Abraham He confirmed it by an oath that by two immutable things (His promise and His oath) He bound Himself irrevocably to its fulfillment. The promises of the Abrahamic Covenant can never be annulled (Galatians 3:15-17).

D. The Book of the Covenant

Though there is no specific mention of the writing of a book in connection with this covenant, in due time, God inspired Moses to give the account of it when he wrote the first five books of the Bible, particularly Genesis and Exodus.

II. The BLOOD of the Covenant

A. The Sacrifice of the Covenant

The sacrificial elements of the Abrahamic Covenant were progressively unfolded during Abraham's life-time.

1. The Bread and Wine (Genesis 14:18)

When Melchisedek appeared to Abraham at the time of the covenant he blessed him and ministered to him the "communion" of bread and wine, which New Testament Scripture shows to be symbolic of the body and blood of Jesus Christ (Matthew 26:26-28).

2. The Animal Sacrifices (Genesis 15:7-17)

When God was giving the covenant promises to Abraham He commanded him to sacrifice five specific offerings. These were an heifer, a she-goat, a ram, a turtledove and a young pigeon. He was to divide the animals in half and lay the pieces, with the birds, in two rows. God Himself, as a burning lamp and smoking furnace, passed between the pieces of the sacrificial body and blood and thus ratified the promises of the covenant (Jeremiah 34:18,19). The particular instructions God gave concerning the covenant sacrifices were later confirmed and expanded in the five offerings of the Mosaic Covenant (Leviticus 1-7). All of these sacrifices were fulfilled and abolished in the perfect sacrifice of Christ on Calvary (Hebrews 10:1-10).

3. The Sacrifice of Isaac (Genesis 22)

God also asked Abraham to offer a "human" sacrifice. He was told to offer his son Isaac as a burnt offering after three days journey to Mount Moriah, The supreme test of faith and obedience was passed by Abraham in this act and God opened his eyes to offer a ram as a substitute for his only son. Thus God the Father led father Abraham to do typically with his only begotten son, Isaac, on Mt Moriah, what He Himself as the Father would do actually with His only begotten Son, Jesus, on Mt Calvary (Hebrews 11:17-19; James 2:20-23).

B. The Mediator of the Covenant

1. The Priesthood of Melchisedek

When Abraham was returning from the slaughter of the kings he was met by Melchisedek who was "priest of the most high God" (Genesis 14). Melchisedek was not only a priest but was also a king, "King of Righteousness and King of Peace." He blessed Abraham, ministered to him the bread and wine and received tithes from him. Subsequent Scripture shows that Christ's king-priesthood is after the order of Melchisedek (Psalms 110; Hebrews 7).

2. The Priesthood of Abraham

The patriarchal priesthood that began with Adam, Noah and Job continued through the fathers, Abraham, Isaac and Jacob unto the Levitical priesthood. The fact that Abraham built an altar and offered sacrifices in obedience to God shows that he was priest of his household (Genesis 15). He also exercised his priestly ministry in his intercession for Lot (Genesis 18-19).

C. The Sanctuary of the Covenant

In that the altar was the place where the priest offered his sacrifice, it constituted the sanctuary of the patriarchs. This altar became God's meeting place with the fathers where He appeared to them and blessed them in connection with the sacrifice (Exodus 20:24-26).

Thus we have the following:

*   Abraham's altar, where he called on the name of the Lord (Genesis 12:7,8; 13:1-4,18; 22:9).

*   Isaac's altar, where he called on the name of the Lord (Genesis 26:25).

*   Jacob's altar, where the Lord appeared unto him (Genesis 33:20; 35:1-15).

The altar was later on incorporated into the Mosaic Covenant economy in the Tabernacle of Moses (Exodus 27:1-9).

III. The SEAL of the Covenant

The Abrahamic Covenant was called the "covenant of circumcision" because its seal was the rite of circumcision (Acts 7:8).

It was referred to as:

*   A Token (Genesis 17:11).

*   A Seal (Romans 4:11).

*   A Sign (Romans 4:11).

A. The Administration of the Rite

In administering the rite of circumcision, three things were involved:

1. The cutting off of the flesh, involving shedding of blood (Genesis 17:9-11).

2. The invocation of the name of the child (Genesis 21:4; Luke 1:59; 2:21).

3. The eighth day (Genesis 17:12; Luke 1:59; 2:21).

B. The Significance of the Rite

Only by obedience to the Commandment of circumcision could any of Abraham's seed be in covenantal relationship with God and entitled to the promises, the privileges and the blessings of the covenant. To reject or neglect this rite would be to break the covenant and to cut himself off from its benefits (Genesis 17:14). Circumcision was the outward evidence of their inward commitment to the terms of the covenant.

C. The Importance of the Rite

So important was the rite of circumcision that God sought to kill Moses for failing to bring his own family into covenantal relationship with God by circumcision. Moses could not deliver God's people Israel on the basis of the Abrahamic Covenant when his own family did not have the seal of that covenant (Exodus 2:23-25; 3:1-6; 4:24-26).

So important was this rite that no Israelite or stranger could partake of the Passover Feast unless they had the seal of circumcision (Exodus 12:43-51).

D. The Fulfillment of the Rite

Though the Abrahamic Covenant focused on the external aspect of circumcision, the New Covenant focuses on its internal application. Even the Old Testament prophets reflected the New Testament reality (Deuteronomy 10:16; 30:6; Jeremiah 4:4; 6:10; Ezekiel 44:7).

1. Fulfillment in Christ

a. In His Experience as an Infant (Luke 2:21)

(1) The rite of circumcision.

(2) The eight day.

(3) The naming of the child, Jesus.

b. In His Baptism at Jordan (Luke 3:21-23)

(1) Into the water—pointing to His death.

(2) Out of the water—pointing to His resurrection.

(3) Receiving the name Christ—pointing to His exaltation.

   c. **In His Experience at Calvary** (Acts 2:22-36).

(1) His crucifixion—cutting off; His broken body and shed blood.

(2) His resurrection—the eighth day.

(3) His exaltation—the exalted name, LORD, received.

  2. Fulfillment in Christians

   a. **In Water Baptism** (Matthew 28:19,20; Acts 2:36-41; Colossians 2:11-13).

(1) Into the water—identification with His death.

(2) Out of the water—identification with His resurrection.

(3) In the name—invocation of the Godhead name.

   b. **In Circumcision of the Heart** (Colossians 2:11-13; Romans 6:14).

(1) Cutting off of the fleshly life.

(2) Experiencing newness of life.

(3) Walking in the nature of the name of the Lord Jesus Christ.

The seal of circumcision of the Abrahamic Covenant is fulfilled in the New Covenant circumcision of the heart. New Covenant circumcision is not of the flesh, but of the heart; not of the letter but of the Spirit; not made by hands externally but made by the Spirit inwardly, whose praise is not of men but whose praise is of God (Romans 2:24-29).

Abraham believed God both when he was uncircumcised and circumcised. Thus he is the father of all who believe, whether the Circumcision or the Uncircumcision. This confirms the truth of the matter that God's desire is for the new creature that is circumcised in heart (Romans 4:8-12; Ephesians 2:11-13; Galatians 6:15,16).

SUMMARY

The general promise of the Adamic Covenant concerning the Messianic seed of the woman which was narrowed down to the race of Shem under the Noahic Covenant was

narrowed further to Abraham, who would becom
through whom the Messiah would come. As th
Testament times the Abrahamic Covenant, ei
itself all previous and subsequent covenants
Covenant through Christ and His Church (Gal

40

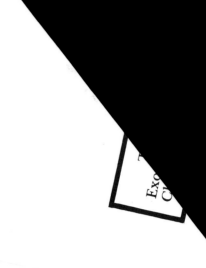

Chapter 6

THE MOSAIC COVENANT

> The Mosaic Covenant was made with the chosen nation, Israel, after the
> Exodus and at Mt Sinai. It was made to be a "schoolmaster" to bring Israel to
> Christ Jesus, the Saviour of the world.

INTRODUCTION

The Mosaic Covenant is the most complicated and the most difficult of all covenants to interpret. The elaborate wording of the covenant, the prolific and intricate details of the sacrifices, priesthood and sanctuary and the complete governing of the national life of Israel by the sabbaths and religious festivals make it the fullest expression of a covenant in Scripture. Its explicit external forms, when rightly interpreted, illustrate the more implicit elements of other covenants. However, both in the early Church and today, much confusion has arisen concerning the purpose of this covenant and its relationship to the other covenants. This is illustrated in Acts 15 and in the Epistles to the Galatian and Hebrew believers.

Why was this covenant given? Did it annul the Abrahamic Covenant? How does the New Covenant affect it? Is it in effect today? How these questions are answered has great theological and eschatological implications.

1. **With whom was the Covenant made?**

    The Mosaic Covenant was made strictly and only with the chosen nation of Israel (Exodus 24:7,8; Deuteronomy 5:1-5; I Kings 8:9,21; Jeremiah 31:31-32; Romans 5:12-14 with John 1:17; Romans 9:4,5).

2. **When was the Covenant given?**

    The Mosaic Covenant was made 430 years after the Abrahamic Covenant (Galatians 3:14-18). It was given to Israel in the wilderness after their deliverance from Egypt. Before this time it was not in effect but was preceded by other covenants of grace and faith.

3. **Why was the Covenant made?**

    There are two parts to the reason why God gave the Mosaic Covenant; that which pertains to Israel's probation and that which pertains to the purpose of God.

    a. **Nation on Probation**

        As Abraham's seed was multiplying and becoming a nation in Egypt, according to the promise, they forsook the Lord and worshipped the idols of Egypt. They failed to maintain their covenantal relationship with the Lord and thus found themselves in bondage (Exodus 1:7-12; Joshua 24:14; Ezekiel 20:5-9).

Exodus 1-4 records the birth and call of Moses who would turn Israel back to God and deliver them from Egyptian bondage. This deliverance was based on the covenant of grace and faith made with their fathers, Abraham, Isaac and Jacob. In remembering the covenant God showed himself to be a covenant-keeping God by revealing His covenant name to Moses and promising to bring Israel into the covenant land (Exodus 2:23-25; 3:6,13-17; 6:1-8). God even gave Moses signs to perform so that Israel would believe in the covenant promises (Exodus 4:1,5,8,9,27-31). However, God sought to kill Moses for failing to maintain the Abrahamic Covenant seal of circumcision in his own family. He could not deliver Israel on the basis of the covenant his own family was not keeping (Genesis 17:9-14; Exodus 4:24-26; Acts 7:8).

Exodus 5-12 records the falling of the ten plagues of judgment on Egypt and the miraculous preservation and deliverance of Israel in connection with the Passover Feast. This was all in fulfilment of the promise God made with Abraham in Genesis 15. On the basis of grace and through their faith and obedience Israel experienced the benefits of the Abrahamic Covenant in their deliverance from Egypt.

This renewal of the Abrahamic Covenant placed the nation on further probation. God took them from Egypt into the Wilderness to prove them and to know what was in their heart (Deuteronomy 8:2,3,15,16). Between Egypt and Sinai God gave them four tests of faith and obedience. In each case they failed. They failed at the test of the Red Sea (Exodus 14:10-12,31). They failed at the test of the waters of Marah (Exodus 15:23-26). They failed at the Wilderness of Sin (Exodus 16:1-12) and they also failed at the test of Rephidim (Exodus 17:1-7).

Though only a few weeks removed from the miracles of Egypt, their ungrateful and murmuring complaints exposed their evil hearts of unbelief (Psalms 78:1-54; 106:1-15). This generation that came out of Egypt proved themselves to be a perverse, crooked and froward generation, "children in whom there is no faith" (Deuteronomy 32:5,20,28,29).

Their subsequent history shows them provoking God ten times (Numbers 14:22). Though they promised God to obey all His commandments (Exodus 19:8; 24:3,7), the Lord lamented the fact that there was no such heart in them to obey (Deuteronomy 5:28,29). Even after receiving the Mosaic Covenant this generation rejected the covenant land and wandered in the Wilderness for 40 years until they all had died (Numbers 13-14 with Hebrews 3-4 and Jude 5). All of this is evidence of the failure of the nation on probation.

In boasting their ability to obey, this generation fell from the ground of grace and faith to the ground of law and works. Thus God gave them a covenant of law and works to expose their helplessness and inability to keep covenant apart from the grace of God.

b.   **World in Court**

Under the Abrahamic Covenant God chose Israel out of the nations to be a model nation through which He could reveal His redemptive purposes, His character and His way of life to other nations (Deuteronomy 5:6-8, 31-40).

In representing all other nations before God, Israel's failure illustrated and confirmed the guilt of all the world, both Jew and Gentile, before God (Romans 3:19).

Through the Mosaic Covenant God brought the whole world into the "court-room" of His just judgment where the Divine attributes of righteousness, truth, mercy and peace were to be revealed. This judgment was actually to prepare the way for the New Covenant. Following are twelve aspects to the Divine purpose for the giving of the Mosaic or the Law Covenant.

(1) To set forth the Divine standard of righteousness (Psalms 19:7-10; Romans 7:12-14).

(2) To give a clear external definition of sin because of the inadequacy of man's conscience (Romans 3:20; 7:7; I John 3:4).

(3) To show Israel the exceeding sinfulness and deceitfulness of sin (Romans 7:11-13; Galatians 3:19).

(4) To expose to all men their guilt before God (Romans 3:19).

(5) To preserve the nation of Israel and the chosen Messianic seed line from total corruption by other nations (Galatians 3:19).

(6) To shut Israel up as a nation "in custody" under a schoolmaster and thus prepare them for Christ's coming (Galatians 3:22-25; 4:1-3).

(7) To illustrate the two major ways of God's dealings with man, which are seen in perfect balance in His own being; Law and Grace (John 1:17).

(8) To foreshadow and typify all the truths of grace and redemption in the ceremonial law, and to typify the person and the work of Christ (Romans 2:20; Hebrews 10:1; Colossians 2:17).

(9) To provide in the ceremonial law a temporary atonement (covering) for sin by which Israel could approach God in worship and upon the basis of which He could dwell in their midst (Hebrews 9-10).

(10) To illustrate more fully and clearly in visible and temporal form all the elements involved in covenantal revelation (Romans 2:20).

(11) To show all the world that none can be justified (made righteous) by the Law, but only through grace and faith (Romans 3:19-22; 9:30-32; 10:1-6; Galatians 3:10-16).

(12) To show that the Law Covenant could not give life, but that only the New Covenant "in Christ" could (Galatians 3:12 with Leviticus 18:5).

4.   **What is the Relationship of the Mosaic Covenant to the Abrahamic Covenant?**

In the early Church there was much confusion concerning the relationship of three great covenants; the Abrahamic, the Mosaic and the New Covenants. Paul gave the solution by pinpointing the relationship of the Mosaic Covenant to the Abrahamic Covenant. The five parts to this answer that are given in the Epistles are listed below:

a.   The Mosaic Covenant did not *annul* nor replace the promises of the Abrahamic Covenant. The Abrahamic Covenant had been made irrevocable by its promises being confirmed with an oath (Galatians 3:8,9,14-18; Hebrews 6:13-20).

b.   The Mosaic Covenant was *added* to or "placed alongside" the Abrahamic Covenant because of Israel's transgressions (Galatians 3:19).

c.   The Mosaic Covenant once instituted was to *run parallel* or co-exist with the Abrahamic Covenant. For this reason the prophets spoke of the covenants co-existing in their day (Galatians 3:15-19; Ezekiel 16:59-63). The Mosaic Covenant and the Abrahamic Covenant both flow into the cross; their ceremonial elements being fulfilled and abolished and their spiritual and eternal elements being fulfilled in the New Covenant.

d.   The Mosaic Covenant was imposed or "laid upon" Israel to prefigure the person and work of Christ (Hebrews 9:9,10).

e.   The Mosaic Covenant was *temporal,* given until Christ the seed of Abraham would come and until the time of reformation which would be brought about by the New Covenant (Galatians 3:19; Hebrews 9:10).

The Abrahamic Covenant, which was everlasting and irrevocable, was not annulled by the Mosaic Covenant, which was temporarily imposed upon Israel until the time when the New Covenant would fulfil the Abrahamic Covenant and abolish the Mosaic Covenant. Thus the Abrahamic Covenant was the transcending eternal covenant while the Mosaic Covenant was the temporary additional covenant.

I.   **The WORDS of the Covenant**

The Mosaic Covenant contains more words than any other covenant given in Old Testament times. Numerous chapters are given to record the words of this covenant (Exodus 20-40; Leviticus 1-27; Numbers 1-10,15,18,19,28,29,30-36), Deuteronomy 1-34). All these words could be classified under the three major divisions of the Law; Moral, Civil and Ceremonial.

*   **The Moral Law**

This consisted of the Ten Commandments written on two tables of stone. These were particularly called "His Covenant" and "The Ten Words" (Deuteronomy 4:13,23; 10:1-5). The Ten Commandments set forth the Divine righteous standard of morality for human conduct in relation to both God and man (Exodus 20; 34:27,28).

*   **The Civil Law**

This multiplied variety of regulations were simply amplifications of the basic principles stated in the Moral Law (Exodus 21-23 being sample chapters). These applications of law governed every area of Israel's life; civilly, socially, economically, personally and legally.

*   **The Ceremonial Law**

This detailed and explicit set of laws governing the sacrifices, the priesthood, the sanctuary and the festival occasions provided atonement for the sins and uncleanness of Israel, individually and nationally. It foreshadowed the person and work of Christ in grace.

A.   **The Promises of the Covenant**

1.   **Promises of Blessing**

In that Israel was to receive the promises of blessing in the Abrahamic Covenant, the Mosaic Covenant was primarily an addition of conditions to the receiving of those blessings. While the Abrahamic Covenant was primarily a covenant of promise the Mosaic Covenant was primarily one of conditions. Thus the statements of promise found in the words of the Mosaic Covenant are actually affirmations of the promises God made in the Abrahamic Covenant. These promises involve personal, national, geographical and spiritual blessings (Exodus 23:25-33; Leviticus 25,26).

2. Promises of Cursing

Though no specific curses are uttered at Mt Sinai, the consequences of unbelief and the punishments for disobedience were clearly spelled out to the first generation out of Egypt (Exodus 22:22-24; Leviticus 26:14-46). Though the prophet Balaam could not curse Israel, whom God had blessed, they could bring the curse of punishment upon themselves by breaking the conditions of the covenant (Numbers 22,23,24; Galatians 3:10). The curses of the broken covenant were fully spelled out in the curses of the Palestinian Covenant which was given to the second generation as an extension of the Mosaic Covenant.

B. The Terms of the Covenant

In that the Mosaic Covenant was primarily adding conditions to the irrevocable promises of the Abrahamic Covenant, it is filled with numerous "ifs" which become the terms of the covenant. Though under previous covenants the terms involved an obedience that arose out of faith, under this covenant the term was an obedience that arose out of the works of self-effort. Thus faith obedience was replaced with legal obedience (Leviticus 18:5; Galatians 3:10-12). Under this covenant Israel could obtain the promise of life only by fulfilling the works of the law to obtain righteousness (Deuteronomy 6:25; Leviticus 18:5; Romans 10:1-5; Galatians 3:21). However, under other covenants they could receive righteousness by faith in God's promises and therefore be able to do His will (Galatians 3:11; Romans 4:1-5). The Mosaic Covenant said "Do and therefore live" while the New Covenant says "Receive life and therefore do". The Mosaic Covenant promoted righteousness by works rather than righteousness by faith.

It was Israel's arrogant self-confidence that provoked God to impose these kinds of terms upon them. Israel boasted "All that the Lord hath said, we will do" and thus moved themselves off the ground of faith to the ground of law and works (Exodus 19:7-9; 24:3,7; Deuteronomy 5:26-29). In doing this Israel as a nation showed their ignorance of God's righteousness, and for 1500 years tried to establish their own righteousness by the Law, refusing to submit themselves to the faith righteousness of the Abrahamic Covenant (Romans 10:1-3; Philippians 3:6-9; Isaiah 64:6). The following is a summary of the terms of the Mosaic Covenant:

1. The Ten Commandments (Exodus 20:1-17; Deuteronomy 5:1-21)

The Ten Commandments were written on two tables of stone, one listing the commandments governing man's relationship to God and the other concerning man's relationship to man. They are called "The Ten Words".

a. Relationship to God

(1) No other gods before Him.

(2) No graven images to be made or worshipped.

       (3) No taking the name of the Lord in vain.

       (4) Keep the Sabbath day holy to the Lord.

  b. **Relationship to Man**

       (1) Honor father and mother.

       (2) No murder.

       (3) No adultery.

       (4) No stealing.

       (5) No False witness.

       (6) No coveting.

2. Obedience

The giving of these commandments automatically required Israel's obedience to them. This was a legal obedience which demanded strict adherence to the commandments. If they obeyed the commandments there was blessing but if they disobeyed there was a curse (Deuteronomy 11:26-28; 13:4; Jeremiah 11:1-10).

3. Love

The only heart that this kind of obedience could arise from was a heart of love for the Lord (Deuteronomy 6:4-6; 10:12,13,16; 30:6-8). It was only as they loved, feared and served the Lord that they would be able to perfectly obey His commandments.

The heart condition required to be able to perfectly fulfill these terms of keeping God's commandments out of loving obedience was not within Israel's reach because of the law of sin that was at work in their hearts (Deuteronomy 5:28,29; Romans 7:7-22). Israel's history under the Mosaic Covenant proved that unless God changed man's heart he would never be able by self-effort to develop a perfect heart of loving obedience toward the Lord. Their failure to keep the law was intended to prepare them for the New Covenant which would bring them "a new heart and a new spirit" and would enable them to obey God (Ezekiel 36:24-27). While the Mosaic Covenant commandments were written externally on tables of stone by the finger of God, the New Covenant commandments are written internally on the tables of our heart and mind by the spirit of God (Jeremiah 31:31-34; Hebrews 8; II Corinthians 3). The Mosaic Covenant gave commandments to keep, but no power to keep them, while the New Covenant not only gives the standards of God's righteousness but also the changing and enabling power of God to fulfill them (Romans 8:1-6). Human effort alone could never accomplish what could only be done by the grace and Spirit of God.

C. The Oath of the Covenant

The Mosaic Covenant was not made irrevocable by a confirming oath. This sets it in contrast with the Abrahamic Covenant which was made everlasting and irrevocable by the giving of an oath (Galatians 3:15-17; Hebrews 6:13-17).

D. The Book of the Covenant

The Scriptures record that this covenant was specifically written in a book. This "book of the covenant" was sprinkled with blood, and was to be read in the audience of the people. It was later placed in the side of the Ark of the Covenant (Exodus 24:7,8; Hebrews 9:19,20; Deuteronomy 31:24-26).

II. The BLOOD of the Covenant

A. The Sacrifice of the Covenant

The Mosaic Covenant has the fullest and most detailed description of sacrifices of any covenant. This illustrates the significance of the sacrifice of a covenant and typifies the importance of the atoning work of Christ.

1. The Body

A careful study of the sacrificial ritual reveals how exacting God was about what happened to the body of the sacrifice. At times the body was to be burnt upon the altar. At other times it was to be burnt outside the camp. On other occasions God, the priest and the offerer shared portions of the body of the sacrificial victim. These complex requirements find their fulfilment in the sacrifice of the body of Jesus (Matthew 26:26-28; Hebrews 10:1-10; 13:11-14).

2. The Blood

God was also very particular about how the sacrificial blood was handled. At times the blood was sprinkled upon the furnishings of the Tabernacle, though most often it was upon the brazen altar. On the Day of Atonement the blood was brought within the veil and sprinkled upon the Mercy seat. These rituals find their fulfilment in the blood of Jesus (Matthew 26:26-28; Hebrews 9; 13:11-14).

3. The Offerings

a. The Five Offerings (Leviticus 1-7).

(1) The Burnt Offering (2) The Meal Offering (3) The Peace Offering	Voluntary Offerings
(4) The Sin Offering (5) The Trespass Offering	Compulsory Offerings

b. The Two Birds for the cleansing of leprosy (Leviticus 13,14).

c. The Daily Sacrifices (Numbers 28:1-8).

d. The Sabbath Day Sacrifices (Numbers 28:9,10).

e. The Festival Sacrifices (Leviticus 16:23; Numbers 28,29).

f. The Sacrifice of the Red Heifer and the Waters of Purification (Numbers).

This elaborate sacrificial system with its multiplied continual sacrifices was given for two major reasons. First, it was to illustrate that no amount of continued animal sacrifices could effectively take away man's sinfulness. Second, it was to point to Christ's perfect, sinless and once-for-all sacrifice that could take away man's sinfulness (Hebrews 9,10). It was the multiplicity of sacrifices that caused the Mosaic Covenant to become known as "the blood covenant" (Zechariah 9:11; Exodus 24:6-8; Hebrews 9:19,20).

There are five major truths which God revealed in the blood of the covenants.

* The blood has a *voice* (Genesis 4:10; Hebrews 12:22-24).

* The blood is the *life* (Genesis 9:4-6; Deuteronomy 12:23).

* The blood is given as an *atonement* for the soul (Leviticus 17:10-14).

* The blood is the evidence of *out-poured life* (Deuteronomy 12:16,23,24).

* The blood is the evidence of *judgment* on sin by death (Exodus 12:13; Leviticus 16:15,16).

B. **The Mediator of the Covenant**

Though the Adamic, Noahic and Abrahamic Covenants were characterized by patriarchal priesthood, the Mosaic Covenant gives the fullest demonstration of priestly service. The mediating priesthood involved two particular persons and then the entire tribe to which they belonged.

1. **Moses**

    Moses, of the tribe of Levi, acted as the *king* of the people of Israel and thus became the mediator of the *words* of the covenant (Deuteronomy 33:15). He was the law-giving mediator between God and Israel (Acts 7:31,38,53; Galatians 3:19,20; Deuteronomy 5:22-27).

2. **Aaron**

    Aaron, also of the tribe of Levi, acted as the *priest* of the people of Israel and thus became the mediator of the *blood* of the covenant (Hebrews 5:1-5). He was the atoning mediator between God and Israel (Exodus 28,29; Leviticus 8,9). It was from Aaron's household that the succession of High Priests ministered for Israel.

3. **Levites**

    Upon Israel's failure to enter into the national priesthood in being "a kingdom of priests", God chose the tribe of Levi to minister before Him (Exodus 19:1-6; Genesis 49:5-7; Deuteronomy 33:8-11; Numbers 3). It was to this tribe that God gave "the covenant of priesthood" (Malachi 2:4-10; Nehemiah 13:29; Numbers 25:10-13). The Book of Leviticus was given primarily to describe their priestly duties and ministrations in relation to the people, the sacrifices and the sanctuary of the Lord.

    The dual king-priesthood of Moses and Aaron prefigured the Priesthood of Christ after the Order of Melchisedek (Hebrews 3:1; 5:1-5; Psalms 110; Hebrews 7). The Levitical Priesthood prefigured the priesthood of all believers in Christ (I Peter 2:5-9; Revelation 5:5-9; 1:6).

    At the time of the New Covenant a great company of Levitical priests became obedient to the faith and thus entered into the Melchisedek Priesthood of Christ (Acts 6:7).

C.   **The Sanctuary of the Covenant**

The sacrificial system and the priesthood ministry both centred in the sanctuary of the covenant, the Tabernacle of Moses. All that was illustrated in the Tabernacle of Eden, and the Patriarchal Altars was embodied in the Tabernacle of Moses. The primary purpose for this Tabernacle is expressed in Exodus 25:8; "And let them make Me a sanctuary, that I may dwell among them". The details concerning the building of the Tabernacle are recorded in Exodus 25-40.

1.   **The Most Holy Place**

This inner chamber was the actual dwelling place of God. The only article of furniture it contained was the *Ark of the Covenant*. Upon its blood-stained Mercy seat the very presence and Shekinah glory of God dwelt. God's redemptive covenant name was invoked upon the Ark (Exodus 25:10-22; Numbers 7:89; II Samuel 6:2).

In the Ark were the *Tables of the covenant,* Aaron's rod that budded and the golden pot of manna (Hebrews 9:1-4; Exodus 34:27,28; Deuteronomy 4:13; 9:9-15). In the side of the Ark was the *Book of the covenant* (Exodus 24:7,8; Deuteronomy 31:24-26).

The High Priest entered this place only once each year on the great Day of Atonement (Leviticus 16; Hebrews 9).

2.   **The Holy Place**

This second chamber was before the Holiest of All and was separated from it by a veil. It contained the golden altar of incense, the golden candlestick and the golden table of shewbread (Exodus 40; Hebrews 9:1-2). Aaron's household daily ministered in this place attending to the furniture (Hebrews 9:1,2,6).

3.   **The Outer Court**

This third area, which surrounded the Holy Place and the Most Holy Place, was enclosed by a curtain fence. It contained the brazen altar and the brazen laver, the places of ceremonial cleansing by blood and water (Exodus 27:1-19; 30:17-21). Here the Levitical priesthood performed its daily sacrifices and ceremonial cleansings for themselves and the people (Hebrews 10:1-11).

All that pertained to the sacrifices, priesthood and sanctuary ministrations belonged to that division of the law spoken of as the ceremonial law. This ceremonial law was actually an illustration of the grace of God and a fore-shadowing of the person and work of the Lord Jesus Christ under the New Covenant. The mediatorial work of the High Priest and the blood-stained Mercy seat in the sanctuary covering the moral law were both illustrations of grace under law. It was only on that basis that God could dwell with Israel even under this Mosaic Covenant. At the establishing of the New Covenant by the cross of Christ, all that which pertained to the shadow of the ceremonial law was fulfilled and abolished. The spiritual reality in Christ remains (Colossians 2:14-17; Hebrews 10).

III. **The SEAL of the Covenant**

The sign or seal of the Mosaic Covenant was the weekly Sabbath day. It is distinctly spoken of as a *sign* between God and the nation of Israel (Exodus 31:12-17; Ezekiel 20:10-26; Leviticus 19:30; Nehemiah 9:14; Leviticus 23:3).

The Lord reminded Israel of the fact that He made the heaven and the earth in six days work, and then sanctified the seventh day as a day of rest. This seventh day of rest in creation became the pattern for God requiring the Israelites to work six days and then rest on the seventh day, the holy Sabbath. The Sabbath was to be observed perpetually throughout their generations. Any one who violated the Sabbath would surely be put to death (Exodus 31:16).

A. **The Sabbath in the Old Testament**

There are a number of important facts concerning the seal of the Mosaic Covenant which need to be noted to see how it finds its fulfilment in the New Covenant.

1. There is no mention of keeping the Sabbath day from Adam to Moses. That is, under the Adamic, Noahic, and Abrahamic Covenants we have no mention of the Sabbath for about 2500 years.

2. The first specific mention of keeping Sabbath is found in Exodus 16:23-26 concerning the gathering of the daily manna and this was spoken to the nation of Israel.

3. The keeping of the Sabbath was the fourth commandment of the Decalogue given to Israel at Mt Sinai (Exodus 20:9-11; 31:18).

4. It is the fourth commandment of the Decalogue that God took to be the sign and seal of the Mosaic Covenant (Exodus 31:12-17; Deuteronomy 5:12-15). Each of the covenants had their own sign and seal and God did not take the sign or seal of other covenants and make such the seal of the Mosaic Covenant.

5. Though the ten commandments are spoken of as the Moral Law, the fourth commandment concerning the Sabbath was actually a ceremonial law. It was this "ceremony" that was attached to the Mosaic Covenant as its seal.

6. There were other special Sabbaths given to Israel besides the weekly Sabbath. These Sabbaths were the holy days of the Festivals of Passover, Pentecost and Tabernacles, and these Sabbaths fell in their appointed weeks as well as the weekly seventh day Sabbath (Leviticus 23:7,8,21,24,27-39).

7. Relative to the land of promise, there were Sabbath years also. Every seventh year, and every fiftieth year were Sabbath years of rest for the land. These Sabbaths of rest for the land pertained to the conditions of the Palestinian Covenant (Leviticus 25:1-22).

The tragic history of the chosen nation shows how they failed to keep the Sabbaths, both for the people and the land, thus breaking the sign and seal of the Mosaic and Palestinian Covenants.

The Scripture clearly states that the reason for the Babylonian Captivity was the failure of Israel to keep the Sabbaths of the Lord. The Sabbath days and years became burdensome to them and they despised them and thus brought Divine judgment upon themselves (II Chronicles 36:21; Ezekiel 20:1-26; Nehemiah 13:15-22; Ezekiel 22:8,26; 23:38; Isaiah 56:2,6,13; Jeremiah 17:21-27).

B.   **The Sabbath in the New Testament**

The New Testament shows clearly how the Jews had misinterpreted and corrupted the Sabbath. They crucified their Messiah, the very one who came to bring to them by the New Covenant the reality of the Sabbath of the Mosaic Covenant (Matthew 12:1-9,10-14; John 5:1-18; 9:1-14).

The New Testament also reveals that the Sabbath is fulfilled in Christ and that the believer under the New Covenant is no longer obligated to keep the Mosaic Covenant Sabbaths.

Following are a number of important facts from the New Testament concerning the seal of the Sabbath and its relationship to the New Covenant seal.

1.   Jesus clarified the fact that the Sabbath was made for man and not man for the Sabbath. The day was given for man's benefit, and man was not given for the benefit of the day. Man needs physical rest and recuperation, as well as time for spiritual refreshment (Mark 2:27,28).

2.   Jesus presented Himself as the *Lord* of the Sabbath. He is higher than the keeping of a day. The Jews kept the letter of the Sabbath, with numerous additions, and missed the spirit of the Sabbath, even crucifying the Lord of the Sabbath. They exalted a day of rest above the only person that could give them true rest (Mark 2:27,28).

3.   Even in Old Testament times when Israel kept the Sabbaths God condemned them for their hypocritical observances (Isaiah 1:10-17; Lamentations 2:6), and predicted the cessation of their feast days and Sabbaths (Hosea 2:11). Paul taught that the holy days, new moons and Sabbath days were merely a shadow of things to come and had been abolished at the Cross (Colossians 2:11,16,17).

4.   All of the moral commandments of the Mosaic Covenant are repeated and endorsed in the New Testament, with only one exception, the ceremonial fourth commandment concerning the Sabbath. This "ceremony" was never stated as a requirement for New Testament believers.

5.   Paul clearly tells us that the Old Covenant was old, decaying and ready to vanish away. It was a ministration of death and was to be done away with (II Corinthians 3:1-18; Hebrews 8:6-13). The New Covenant has its own sign and seal, even the true and spiritual rest, which is the baptism in the Holy Spirit (Isaiah 28:9-11; Acts 2:1-4). To take the Sabbath day and impose its keeping upon Christians today, Jew of Gentile, is to take the sign and seal of the Old Covenant and add it to the sign and seal of the New Covenant. It then becomes a confusion of covenants.

6.   Even as the seals of the other covenants find their fulfilment in the seal of the New Covenant, so the Sabbath rest is fulfilled in the New Covenant rest.

The New Testament clearly shows that the seal of the New Covenant is the receiving of the Holy Spirit (Ephesians 1:13,14; 4:30). This is true spiritual rest (Isaiah 28:11,12).

7. In Christ the believer finds true Sabbath rest. He ceases from his own works and rests in the finished work of Christ. It is "in Christ" that there is everlasting rest. This fulfills "the perpetual covenant" of Sabbath rest. It is not in the keeping of *a day* but in the receiving of *a person* — Christ Jesus our Lord — that one finds the rest of God (Matthew 11:28-30).

SUMMARY

The Mosaic Covenant finds its perfect fulfilment in the Lord Jesus Christ. He was the only Man who ever perfectly kept the law in all its requirements. He fulfilled and abolished in His cross all that which pertained to the ceremonials and the externals of the law. That righteousness which is in the law, which is holy, just, good, spiritual and perfect, finds its fulfilment in Christ Himself re-living His sinless life in the believer "who walks not after the flesh but after the Spirit" (Romans 8:1-4). Christ's new law of love to God and man, written on the tablets of the heart, by the Spirit, enable the believer to live that life that is pleasing to God.

Chapter 7

THE PALESTINIAN COVENANT

The Palestinian Covenant was made in the land of Moab with the second generation out of Egypt of the chosen nation of Israel. It was given at the end of the forty years wanderings in the wilderness and just before they entered into the land promised in the Abrahamic Covenant. It laid down for all generations the conditions for entering and maintaining the promised land.

INTRODUCTION

Because of its close association with the Mosaic Covenant, the Palestinian Covenant has often not been recognized as a covenant in its own right. However, Deuteronomy 29:1 clearly distinguishes it from the Mosaic Covenant by stating, "beside the covenant which He made with them in Horeb." While the Mosaic Covenant was made at Mt Sinai with the first generation out of Egypt and gave laws for the people, the Palestinian Covenant was made in the plains of Moab with the second generation and gave laws for the land. Thus these are two distinct covenants given in two distinct places to two distinct generations for two distinct reasons.

While this new generation received a new covenant, the Palestinian Covenant, it also received a rehearsal of the Moral and Civil Laws of the Mosaic Covenant. This constitutes the book of Deuteronomy, "The Second Law". Thus this generation was under the Mosaic Covenant, received the Palestinian Covenant and entered the land promised in the Abrahamic Covenant.

The failure of the first generation to keep the Abrahamic and Mosaic Covenants precipitated the giving of the Palestinian Covenant. The climax of their failure is recorded in Numbers 13,14. At Kadesh-Barnea they searched the land for forty days, believed the "evil report" and in unbelief rejected the covenant land promised to Abraham. God transposed the forty days into forty years of wandering in the wilderness to experience His "breach of promise" (Numbers 14:34). Thus, the first generation died in unbelief failing to enter into covenant rest (Hebrews 3,4; Deuteronomy 8:1-16). The old generation experienced the cycle of probation, failure and judgment which led to the new generation receiving the next covenant. The Palestinian Covenant reaffirms and fully amplifies the conditions of the Mosaic Covenant for the keeping of the land promised in the Abrahamic Covenant.

I.   **The WORDS of the Covenant**

The word "land" is used approximately 180 times in the Book of Deuteronomy. This illustrates that the primary focus of the Palestinian Covenant was on the promised land. It was made with the generation that was about to enter into the land, giving them the conditions of living in the land.

A.   **The Promises of the Covenant**

The Book of Deuteronomy gave that generation a graphic description of the promised land. God had distinctly said that it was "His land" (Leviticus 25:23,24) and that He was allowing them to enter into that land as stewards over it. God described this land as:

*   A land of hills and valleys.

*   A land watered by early and latter rains.

*   A land of fruitfulness.

*   A land watched over by the Lord God.

*   ˙A land of rivers and fountains.

*   A land of mineral wealth.

*   A land of prosperity.

   (Deuteronomy 8:7-10; 11:9-17; 26:15; 28:11-13; Leviticus 26:3-13).

1.   **Promises of Blessing** (Deuteronomy 28:1-14)

God promised that if they were obedient many blessings would come upon Israel and overtake them. They would be placed high above all nations. Moses also gave particular blessings to each of the twelve tribes, even as Jacob had blessed each of his twelve sons (Deuteronomy 33 with Genesis 49). Following are the blessings of the Palestinian Covenant:

a.   Blessed in the city.

b.   Blessed in the field.

c.   Blessed in fruitfulness.

d.   Blessed in daily provision.

e.   Blessed in daily activities.

f.   Blessed in victory over their enemies.

g.   Blessed in storehouses.

h.   Blessed in labor.

i.   Blessed in seasonal rains.

j.   Blessed in national position.

k.   Blessed in commerce.

The fulfilment of these promises of blessing began with the ministry of Joshua as he led them in their conquest and possession of the land promised originally in the Abrahamic Covenant and confirmed in the Mosaic and Palestinian Covenants. Joshua records their victory over their enemies and the dividing of the land into the tribal inheritances (Joshua 11:23; 21:43-45). The Books of Judges, Ruth, I and II Samuel, I and II Kings and I and II Chronicles record times when these promises of blessing were fulfilled in the history of Israel. The greatest extent of their conquest came through the leadership of David and the greatest extent of their material prosperity came during the reign of King Solomon.

2. **Promises of Cursing** (Deuteronomy 28:15-68)

God promised that if they were disobedient many cursings would come upon Israel and overtake them. These are distinctly referred to as curses of the covenant, meaning that God would be bound by His word to judge them for their disobedience (I Kings 8; Leviticus 26; Deuteronomy 27:15-26). Following are the curses of the Palestinian Covenant:

a. Cursed in the city.

b. Cursed in the field.

c. Cursed in daily provision.

d. Cursed in fruitfulness.

e. Cursed in daily activities

f. Cursed in labor.

g. Cursed in diseases.

h. Cursed in the land.

i. Cursed in the lack of rains.

j. Cursed in defeat by their enemies.

k. Cursed in captivities.

l. Cursed in domestic life.

m. Cursed in possessions.

n. Cursed in national position.

The fulfilment of these promises of cursing began in the time of the Judges when the people turned away from God to idols and suffered for it (Judges 2). The Books of Ruth, I and II Samuel, I and II Kings and I and II Chronicles record times in which these promises of cursing were fulfilled in the history of Israel. The ultimate fulfilment of these curses in the Old Testament came with the captivities of the houses of Israel and Judah (II Kings; II Chronicles).

B. **The TERMS of the Covenant**

In that God had already stated that "the land is Mine" (Leviticus 25:23,24) He had established the fact of His ownership and rulership over the land. He presented Himself to Israel as the Lord of the land, their "land-lord", and as such He laid down the conditions for their possessing the land. Though under the Abrahamic Covenant the land had been promised as an "everlasting possession" (Genesis 17:8), under the Palestinian Covenant conditions were added that had to be met in order for the promise to be fulfilled. The Palestinian Covenant being attached to the Mosaic Covenant had the same terms as the Mosaic Covenant. However, the overwhelming emphasis in the Palestinian Covenant was on obedience. There had to be obedience to the moral laws as well as the laws of the land. The most specific term attached to this covenant was the keeping of the seventh year and jubilee Sabbath rest for the land. The terms of the covenant were the following:

1. Obedience to the Ten Commandments, even as under the Mosaic Covenant (Deuteronomy 5:1-21). Upon entering Canaan they were to write the words of the covenant on plastered stones (Deuteronomy 27:1-4).

2.   Love for God (Deuteronomy 6:4-6; 10:12-16; 30:6-8).

3.   Rest for the Land.

   a.   Every seventh year was to be a year of rest for the land (Leviticus 25:1-7).

   b.   Every fiftieth year was to be a jubilee year of rest for the land (Leviticus 25:8-17).

   c.   God promised tremendous blessing of fruitfulness in the years of labor to provide for them through these Sabbath years (Leviticus 25:18-22).

The tragic history of Israel reveals their failure to keep the terms of this covenant as well as their judgment by expulsion from the land. God foreknew and foretold this result by Moses even before they entered the land (Deuteronomy 31:15-21). They experienced the curses of the covenant, the sicknesses and plagues of the land, being overthrown like Sodom and Gomorrah, and finally being rooted out of their land and cast into another land because of their forsaking of the covenant as other nations before them (Deuteronomy 29:16-29; Leviticus 18:24-28).

C.   **The Oath of the Covenant**

Though there is no oath attached to the blessings of this covenant, there is an oath attached to its curses. This oath was meant to assure Israel of the certainty and severity of God's punishment upon their covenantal disobedience, even though they were His chosen nation. Daniel 9:11 refers to the oath of this covenant, as being part of the "law of Moses". To properly interpret this it must be remembered that both the Mosaic and Palestinian Covenants were given by Moses and both can be referred to as "his law".

D.   **The Book of the Covenant**

The Book of the Covenant is referred to in Deuteronomy 31:9,10,24-26. Moses was told to write the law in a book and place it in the side of the Ark of the covenant. It was to be there as a witness against Israel. It was to be read especially to Israel every seventh year, or the Sabbath year, and this was to be done during the Feast of Tabernacles, the feast of the seventh month. As other covenants, it finds its place in the Bible, God's Book.

II.   **The BLOOD of the Covenant**

A.   **The Sacrifice of the Covenant**

The Palestinian Covenant sacrifices follow the pattern laid down in the Mosaic Covenant sacrifices.

1.   **The Body**

Moses told Israel that they were to build an altar of unhewn stones on the day that they passed over Jordan into the land. Upon this altar they offered the sacrifices of burnt offerings and peace offerings unto the Lord. The body of the sacrificial victims were presented as voluntary offerings (Deuteronomy 27:5-7 with Leviticus 1,2,3).

2. **The Blood**

The offerings of the burnt and peace offerings involved the shedding of sacrificial blood (Deuteronomy 27:5-7). It was upon the basis of voluntary sacrificial offerings, the body and blood of innocent victims that Israel inherited the land of promise. There could be no land of rest apart from sacrifice.

B. **The Mediator of the Covenant**

The same priesthood established under the Mosaic Covenant was in mediatorial work under the Palestinian Covenant. This is seen in the order of their religious service when Israel entered the land (Deuteronomy 27:1-14; Joshua 8:30-35).

1. **Eleazar**

After the death of the Law giving Mediator, Moses, and the death of the Atoning-Mediator, Aaron, Eleazar was chosen to be the next High Priest. Under Eleazar's priesthood Joshua would receive direction from the Lord concerning the conquest and division of the land into its tribal inheritances (Numbers 27:15-23; Deuteronomy 27:9,10; Joshua 14:1; 17:4). Thus Eleazar was the High Priest during the initial fulfilment of the Palestinian Covenant.

2. **Levites**

Associated with Eleazar the High Priest were the priests and Levites. As the people of Israel stood on the respective mountains of blessing and cursing, the Levites were to declare to all the men of Israel the curses of the Law. The people were to respond with an "Amen". The Levites were to teach the people the laws of God and thus be the mediators of the words of the covenant (Deuteronomy 27:9-26; 33:8-11).

C. **The Sanctuary of the Covenant**

Relative to the Palestinian Covenant, the land itself was considered to be God's sanctuary. In order to appreciate the significance of this fact it is worthy to note the order of the dedicatory service which God, through Moses, commanded Israel to perform the day they entered the promised land. These facts together show how the land of Canaan was the sanctuary of this covenant.

1. Upon Israel's entering the land they were to write the *words* of the covenant on great plastered stones (Deuteronomy 27:1-4; Joshua 8:32).

2. Then upon the altar the *sacrifices* of the covenant were to be offered, thus dedicating the land to God by blood atonement (Deuteronomy 27:5-7; Joshua 8:30,31).

3. The *Ark* of the Covenant was centred between two mountains, Gerizim and Ebal (Joshua 8:33).

4. The priests and the Levites, as *mediators* of the covenant, along with Eleazar stood in their places relative to the Ark of the Lord.

5. The tribes of Israel stood at the Mount of Blessing, Mount Gerizim and the Mount of Cursing, Mount Ebal as the words of the covenant, the blessings and the cursings were read to them by Joshua and confirmed to them by the Levites (Deuteronomy 27:11-14; Joshua 8:34-35).

6. Palestine, the blessed and rich land of promises was spoken of in very glorious terms.

   a. It was the land of *promise* (Genesis 17:8).

   b. It was the *pleasant* land (Daniel 8:9; Psalms 106:24).

   c. It was the *glory* of all lands (Ezekiel 20:6,15).

   d. It was the *glorious* land (Daniel 11:41).

   e. It was *Immanuel's* land (Isaiah 8:8).

   f. It was the land of *rest* (Hebrews 4).

   g. It was the *Sanctuary* land of the Lord (Exodus 15:17; Psalms 78:54).

When God set the boundaries of the inheritances of all other nations, He gave to each their own land but He chose Palestine as "His land", His sanctuary. In this land was "the holy city" (Nehemiah 11:1,18); "the holy hill" (Psalms 15:1); "the holy temple" (Psalms 5:7); "the holy mountains" of Sinai and Zion (Psalms 68:17; 87:1; Daniel 9:16,20). It was to this land the Messiah would come and fulfill the covenants of God. Hence it is spoken of as "the holy land" (Zechariah 2:12).

Thus when God looked down upon all the countries of the earth, the promised land was His Sanctuary, the most holy place, the earth's "Holiest of All", because of God's covenantal purposes which would ultimately lead to the New Covenant and the cross of Jesus Christ.

The scene enacted in Joshua 8 as Israel entered the land included an Altar of Sacrifice, the Ark of the Covenant, the Priesthood, and two mounts of blessing and cursing. This constituted the land as "the sanctuary" of the Palestinian Covenant.

III. The SEAL of the Covenant

There are two parts to the seal of this covenant; the sabbath rest for the land and the early and latter rains.

A. The Sabbath Rest

As the Sabbath day of rest for the people was the seal of the Mosaic Covenant, so the Sabbath year of rest for the land was the seal of the Palestinian Covenant. Every seventh year was to be a year of rest for the land. During that year the Israelites were not to till the land (Leviticus 25:1-7). Also every fiftieth year was to be a jubilee year of rest for the land (Leviticus 25:8-17). This was the part of the seal of the covenant that Israel was responsible to keep.

B. The Early and Latter Rains

Upon Israel's obedience to this covenant God promised to send the early and latter rains as His seal upon the land, the token of His covenant blessings. However, if they failed to keep the terms of the covenant, including rest for the land, God promised to withhold the rains from the land (Leviticus 25:18-22; Deuteronomy 11:10-17; 28:1-8; Kings 8:35-40; Joel 2).

Israel's history reveals their suffering the consequences of breaking both the Mosaic and Palestinian Covenants. Their major violations were their repeated idolatry and immorality as well as their continued failure to keep the Sabbaths (Leviticus 26:33,34; Ezekiel 20:1-26; II Chronicles 36:21).

These sins forced God to judge them by withholding the rains repeatedly through their history and eventually by spewing them out of the land, as He had done to the previous nations (Jeremiah 5:24; Amos 4:6-12; I Kings 17:1; Joel 1; Haggai 1:1-11). The Northern Kingdom of Israel was cast out of the land in 721 B.C. by Assyrian Captivity and never returned to the land as a nation. They were scattered among all nations and were to wander into other lands by God's appointment to fulfill their destiny as seen in the Abrahamic Covenant (Amos 9:8,9; II Samuel 7:10).

The Southern Kingdom of Judah was cast out of the land in 606 B.C. by Babylonian Captivity and returned to the land after 70 years. These 70 years were to make up for the 70 seventh-year Sabbaths in which they had not allowed the land to rest (II Chronicles 36:21). At the close of the 70 year captivity the remnant of Judah was allowed to return to Jerusalem to rebuild the city and the sanctuary (Ezra 1:1-4). God's purpose in this was to hold them in the land until the coming of the Messiah and the establishing of the New Covenant. Ironically, as a nation, they rejected their own Messiah (John 1:11,12). Because of this Jesus foretold the desolation of the city, the temple, the people and their expulsion once again from the land (Luke 19:41-44; 21:20-24; Daniel 9:26; Matthew 23:38; 24:1-2).

With the dispersion of the house of Judah the land itself became desolate, with the cessation of the early and latter rains, for centuries. Just as God was careful to bring a remnant of Judah out of Babylonian Captivity to be in the land for Messiah's first coming, so today God has, as a sign, allowed a remnant of Judah out of all nations to return to the land in preparation for the second coming. The Scriptures indicate that the Jews will receive an outpouring of the Holy Spirit and will be grafted back into the olive tree by faith in the New Covenant in Christ (Zechariah 12; Romans 9,10,11). All of this illustrates the fact that God's covenantal purposes for His natural people centre around the land.

SUMMARY

The Palestinian Covenant is undoubtedly a "land covenant". The land promised in the Abrahamic Covenant and confirmed in the Mosaic Covenant was made conditional under the Palestinian Covenant. Though before the cross the land was exalted geographically and spiritually as the base for God's redemptive purposes for the earth, since the cross the land has ceased to be the focal point for redemption. It is no longer a "holy" land having spiritual elevation. The focal point of redemption is no longer a *promised place* but a *promised person*: Christ (John 4:20-24; Galatians 4:22-31; Revelation 11:8).

The natural language of the Palestinian Covenant is given spiritual significance in the New Testament in relation to the Church. Just as the principles of rest and rain upon obedience to the covenant are applicable to any land or nation naturally, so it is applicable to the Church spiritually. The New Testament speaks of the Church as being God's land which He tills with the expectation of receiving spiritual fruit (I Corinthians 3:9). In this way the outpouring of the early and latter rains represent the outpouring of the Holy Spirit on the Church and upon all flesh (James 5:7; Joel 2:18-32). This also is dependant upon obedience to the terms of the New Covenant.

Chapter 8

THE DAVIDIC COVENANT

> The Davidic Covenant was made with David after the death of Saul and David's enthronement at Jerusalem. It involved David's Seed, House, Throne and Kingdom both naturally and spiritually. It pointed ultimately to the everlasting Throne and Kingdom of the Lord Jesus Christ, David's greatest Son.

INTRODUCTION

The Davidic Covenant is an extension of the Abrahamic Covenant in that the major promises of the Abrahamic Covenant are confirmed and amplified in the Davidic Covenant. It is also a confirmation of the Mosaic Covenant. However, the chief promise of the Davidic Covenant is the promise of kingship. In these prior covenants there was a progressive revelation of kingship.

Kingship was promised in the Abrahamic Covenant:

* To Abraham — The Covenant Father (Genesis 17:6).

* To Sarah — The Covenant Mother (Genesis 17:16).

* To Jacob — The Covenant Father (Genesis 35:11).

* To Judah — The Covenant Tribe (Genesis 49:8-12).

Kingship was promised in the Mosaic Covenant:

* To Israel — The Covenant Nation (Numbers 23:21; Deuteronomy 17:14-20).

Kingship was promised in the Davidic Covenant:

* To David — The Covenant House (II Samuel 7; Psalms 132; I Chronicles 17; Psalms 89).

In its ultimate sense the Davidic Covenant includes in itself the New Covenant because the major promise of kingship of the line of David finds its fulfilment in Jesus Christ, the Son of David. He was promised that He would rule over the house, throne and kingdom of David forever and of "the increase of His government there would be no end" (Luke 1:30-33; Isaiah 9:6-9; Matthew 1:1).

The relationship of the Abrahamic, Davidic and New Covenants is clearly seen in the promise of kingship that culminated in the Messiah, the Lord Jesus Christ. To Him was given the "key of David" (Isaiah 22:20-25; Revelation 3:7-13).

An understanding of the linking promises in these covenants reveals that it was God's will that Israel have a theocratic monarchy to establish them as a nation and kingdom. However, as seen in the "probation cycle", Israel failed to wait for God's will and time in the establishing of the kingdom. While under the probation of the Mosaic and Palestinian Covenants, and while developing as a nation, Israel's form of government was theocratic. God, as their king, sovereignly raised up ministries to lead them, beginning with Moses and Joshua and continuing through the Judges until Samuel, who was priest, judge and prophet. However, during this time there was the recognition of the need for a godly king (Judges 17:6; 18:1; 19:1; 21:25). Without a king to command them Israel wandered away from the Lord into idolatry, immorality, violence, rebellion and anarchy (Judges 17-21).

It was in the time of the failure of both the people and the priesthood that God raised up Samuel the prophet (I Samuel 1-6). However, though Samuel was a godly man his sons as judges over Israel became perverse in their judgments (I Samuel 8:1-4). This precipitated the people's rejection of Samuel's household and their premature desire for a king to judge them. In desiring the kind of king that other nations had they impatiently rejected God's kind of kingship which He desired to give them (I Samuel 8:5-8). Though it was not God's perfect will, He permitted them to have a king and chose Saul of the tribe of Benjamin (I Samuel 8:9-18; 9:10).

It was God's will for them to have a king, but it was not His time nor was Saul from the tribe having the covenant promise of kingship (Genesis 49:10). The Abrahamic Covenant promise of the land was fulfilled 40 years late because of Israel's unbelief (Numbers 13,14). The Abrahamic Covenant promise of a king was precipitated 40 years early because of Israel's impatience. It was after the 40 years reign of Saul and the enthronement of David over all Israel that God made this covenant with David.

I.   **The WORDS of the Covenant**

Though the full words and details of the Davidic Covenant were not given until David was anointed king over all Israel, certain words of the promises of his kingship were given at his anointing by Samuel and during the period of his rejection under the reign of Saul (II Samuel 3:1,9,10). This is seen in the following:

*   The Lord told Samuel the prophet to anoint David the shepherd to be the future king. The Spirit of the Lord came upon David from that day forward (I Samuel 15:28; 16:1-13; 28:17).

*   The men of Achish spoke of David as being the king of the land (I Samuel 21:11).

*   Jonathan knew also that David would be king over Israel in due time (I Samuel 23:17).

*   King Saul also knew that David would be king over Israel (I Samuel 24:20).

*   The men of Judah came and anointed David king over the House of Judah. This was David's second anointing (II Samuel 2:1-4).

*   In due time all the elders of Israel anointed David as king over all Israel. This was David's third anointing (II Samuel 5:1-5).

Thus it was to David, the man after God's own heart that the final covenant of the Old Testament era was given. The next covenant to be revealed was the New Covenant.

The primary chapters of Scripture that contain the elements of the Davidic Covenant are II Samuel 7; I Chronicles 17; Psalms 89; Psalms 132 and Jeremiah 33.

A.   **The Promises of the Covenant**

1.   **Promises of Blessing**

a.   **Appointed Land** (II Samuel 7:10; I Chronicles 17:9).

Even though in David's time Israel was dwelling in the Abrahamic

Covenant land God promised that they would be planted in an ordained place. They would move no more nor be wasted as they had been both in Egypt and in Canaan. This would happen after the "rooting up" referred to in I Kings 14:15. This was particularly fulfilled in relation to the House of Israel in their Assyrian Captivity and wandering among all nations to their newly appointed place and "promised land" (Amos 9:8,9).

Note:— Refer the "land" promises in the Abrahamic and Palestinian Covenants.

b. **Victory over Enemies** (II Samuel 7:11; I Chronicles 17:10).

This promise is an extension of the promise God made to Abraham that his seed would "possess the gate of his enemies" (Genesis 22:17; 24:60). This began with the conquests of Joshua, continued with the tribe of Judah and was consummated naturally with David's victories over all his enemies (Joshua 11,12; Judges 1; II Samuel 8; I Chronicles 22:8). David not only regained territory that had been lost but he also conquered all the land promised to Abraham (II Chronicles 9:26). His victories pointed to the spiritual victory of Christ, the Lion of the tribe of Judah, and of the Church (Revelation 5:5; Matthew 16:18).

c. **Ruling Dynasty** (II Samuel 7:11-16; I Chronicles 17:11-15).

This promise is also an extension of the Abrahamic Covenant promises of kingship (Genesis 17:6,16; 35:11; 49:10). God promised David that He would build his household by establishing his seed upon his throne to rule over his kingdom forever.

(1) Davidic Seed — his descendants.

(2) Davidic House — his dynasty.

(3) Davidic Throne — his authority.

(4) Davidic Kingdom — his dominion.

Under the Abrahamic Covenant God chose a nation (Israel) and from the nation He chose a tribe (Judah). Under the Davidic Covenant He chose a family (David of Jesse) from the tribe (Genesis 17:6,16; 49:8-12; Psalms 78:67-72; 89:3,4). This promise finds its fulfilment in the unbroken dynasty of Davidic kings from Solomon to Zedekiah in the promised land.

Note: None of the Kings of the House of Israel were of the Davidic Seed.

The Dynasty of David:

(1) Solomon — I Kings 1-11.

(2) Rehoboam — I Kings 12-14.

(3) Abijam — I Kings 15:1-8; II Chronicles 13:1-22.

(4) Asa — I Kings 15; II Chronicles 14,15,16.

(5) Jehosaphat — I Kings 15:24; II Chronicles 17,18,19,20.

(6) Jehoram — I Kings 22:50; II Kings 8:16-24; II Chronicles 21.

(7) Ahaziah—II Kings 8:24-29; 9:27; II Chronicles 22:1-9.

(8) Joash—II Kings 11:4-21; II Chronicles 22,23,24.

(9) Amaziah—II Kings 12:21; 14:1-20; II Chronicles 24,25.

(10) Uzziah—II Kings 14,15; II Chronicles 26.

(11) Jotham—II Kings 15:32-38; II Chronicles 27.

(12) Ahaz—II Kings 15:38; 16:1-2-; II Chronicles 28.

(13) Hezekiah—II Kings 18,19,20; II Chronicles 28,30,31,32.

(14) Manasseh—II Kings 21:1-18; II Chronicles 33.

(15) Amon—II Kings 21; II Chronicles 33:20-25.

(16) Josiah—II Kings 22,23; II Chronicles 34,35.

(17) Jehoahaz—II Kings 23:31-34; II Chronicles 36:1-4.

(18) Jehoiakim—II Kings 23:34-37; 24:1-6; II Chronicles 36:4-8.

(19) Jehoiachin—II Kings 24:6-17; II Chronicles 36:8-10.

(20) Zedekiah—II Kings 24:17-20; 25; II Chronicles 36:10-21.

Zedekiah was the last Davidic king to reign over the House of Judah in the land of Canaan. His reign ended with the destruction of Jerusalem and the temple, the captivity of Judah to Babylon and the death of the royal sons. This is the end of the Biblical record of the national Davidic throne. However, this seemed to contradict the promise God had made to David that his seed, house, throne and kingdom would endure as the sun and the moon remained (Psalms 89:3,4,29-39; 132:11,12; Jeremiah 33:17-26).

Regardless of whatever theorizing is done concerning this, the New Testament is clear that Jesus is the ultimate fulfillment of the dynastic promise to David. Gabriel declared ". . . and the Lord God shall give unto him the throne of his father David; and he shall reign over the House of Jacob forever; and of his kingdom there shall be no end" (Luke 1:32,33). (See also Acts 2:29-36.)

d. **Sure Mercies** (II Samuel 7:15; I Chronicles 17:13)

God promised David that if his seed committed iniquity He would chastise them but not take His mercy away from them as He did in cutting off the household of Saul by death. For this reason David continually spoke of the covenant mercy of the Lord (Psalms 51:1; 56:1; 57:1-3). The Davidic Covenant psalm also speaks of the mercy of the Lord (Psalms 89:1,2,14,28-34).

The New Testament shows the ultimate fulfillment of the sure mercies of David to be the resurrection of Jesus from the dead as well as the resurrection of all believers (Acts 13:34; II Timothy 2:8; Revelation 20:6).

e. **Messianic Seed** (II Samuel 7: 11-16; I Chronicles 17: 11-5)

As an extension of the Abrahamic Covenant this is the final covenant "seed promise" of the Old Testament era. The seed of David finds its fulfillment ultimately in the Lord Jesus Christ. He was David's Lord and Root as to His Divinity but was David's son and offspring as to His humanity. The writer to the Hebrews applied the "father-son" clause of the Davidic Covenant to Jesus Christ (II Samuel 7:14 with Hebrews 1:5).

(1) A virgin of the House of David would bring forth Immanuel (Isaiah 7:13,14).

(2) A Righteous Branch would be raised up to David (Jeremiah 25:5,6; 33:15).

(3) Jesus Christ is the son of Abraham and the son of David (Matthew 1:1; Acts 13:22,23).

(4) He is the seed of David after the flesh (Romans 1:3,4).

(5) He is the root and offspring of David (Revelation 22:16).

(6) He is the lion of the tribe of Judah (Revelation 5:5).

(7) He is to receive the throne of His father David and reign over the house of Jacob forever so that His kingdom shall have no end (Luke 1:31-33; Isaiah 9:6-9). He will have an eternal ruling dynasty.

f. **The Temple** (II Samuel 7:13; I Chronicles 17:11-15).

It was David's desire to build a house for God that prompted the giving of the Davidic Covenant (II Samuel 7:1-10; I Chronicles 17:1-10). Though David wanted to build God's house, God promised that He would build David a house by raising up his seed as an enduring dynasty. He would, however, allow David's son to build a house for His name. This house became known as the Temple of Solomon (I Chronicles 28,29; II Chronicles 2:1) and prefigured to Christ and His Church (John 2:18-21; I Corinthians 3:16; Ephesians 2:19-22; I Timothy 3:15).

2. Promises of Cursing

Like the Abrahamic Covenant, the Davidic Covenant was primarily a covenant of blessing having no curse attached to it. However, some kings of the Davidic line did bring judgment upon themselves by their willful transgressions and violations of the terms of the covenant (II Chronicles 36; Jeremiah 22:18-30).

B. The Terms

1. Faith

David was a man of faith having a responsive heart to the word of God (Romans 4:6-8; Psalms 27:13; Hebrews 11:32-34). The covenant God made with him required a faith response to see it fulfilled. After David received the covenant words he worshipped the Lord, expressing his covenant faith (II Samuel 7:18-29; I Chronicles 17:16-27). God expected David's descendants to continue in the faith of David.

2. Obedience

God's testimony concerning David was that he was "a man after Mine own heart, which shall fulfill all My will" (Acts 13:22). The covenant God made with David required obedience to His word (II Samuel 7:14; Psalms 89:30-33; 132:11,12). Upon disobedience God could transfer the throne to another of the seed of David as He said in a warning to Solomon (II Chronicles 7: 12-22).

C. The Oath of the Covenant

Being a part of the Abrahamic Covenant, the Davidic Covenant was confirmed with an oath which made its promises irrevocable (Psalms 89:3-5,27-35; 132:11; II Samuel 3:9,10). Though God promised to chasten David's seed for their transgressions He also vowed to remember His mercy. There could be chastisement of the covenant kings but not abrogation of the covenant promises (II Samuel 7:14,15; Psalms 89:30-34).

The ultimate fulfillment of this oath was fulfilled in the sinless Christ of God, the Son of David, who received the oath of eternal kingship (Acts 2:29-35).

D. The Book of the Covenant

Although there is no specific mention of the writing of a book in connection with this covenant, it was recorded under inspiration of the Holy Spirit in due time in the Books of II Samuel, I Chronicles and Psalms.

II. The BLOOD of the Covenant

In relation to the Sacrifice, Priesthood and Sanctuary, the inter-relatedness of the Davidic Covenant with other Covenants must be recognized. As a covenant man, David was particularly under the Abrahamic Covenant, the Mosaic Covenant, the Palestinian Covenant and the Davidic Covenant. His relationship to the Mosaic and the Davidic must be particularly distinguished.

* In relation to the *Sacrifices,* according to the Mosaic Covenant, David could not offer the compulsory offerings. However, under the Davidic Covenant he did offer the sacrifices of thanksgiving and praise, as well as voluntary offerings.

* In relation to the *Priesthood,* David could not participate in the Levitical priesthood of the Mosaic Covenant but he could act as a king-priest in relation to the Davidic Covenant.

* In relation to the *Sanctuary,* David did not despise the Tabernacle of Moses of the Mosaic Covenant at Gibeon, but he did establish the Tabernacle of David of the Davidic Covenant at Zion.

A. The Sacrifice of the Covenant

As with all redemptive covenants before the cross, animal body and blood constituted the sacrifice of the Davidic Covenant. However, this covenant also involved spiritual sacrifices like that of the coming New Covenant.

1. The Body

When David brought the Ark of the Covenant to Jerusalem he offered the voluntary burnt offerings and peace offerings before the Lord (II Samuel 6:17,18; I Chronicles 16:1-3). The bodies of these sacrificial victims were presented to God as free-will offerings in this dedicatory service (Leviticus 1,3).

2. The Blood

The burnt and peace offerings involved the shedding of sacrificial blood. The authority of the king was to be based on blood atonement (II Samuel 6:17,18; I Chronicles 16:1-3).

3. Spiritual Sacrifices

Though David offered animal sacrifices according to the requirements of the Mosaic Covenant, he also offered the spiritual sacrifices of praise and thanksgiving under the Davidic Covenant. These later became part of the New Covenant order of worship (Psalms 27:6; 141:1; 116:17-19; Hebrews 13:15,16; I Peter 2:5).

B. The Mediator of the Covenant

The priesthood of this Covenant involved David acting as King-Priest as well as the involvement of the Levitical priesthood in the Tabernacle of David.

1. David—The King-Priest

Although David was not a priest after the Levitical order, he did act in the order of Melchisedek. The evidence of David touching this priesthood is shown in the following.

    a. David wore a linen ephod, a priestly garment, symbolic of righteousness (II Samuel 6:14; I Chronicles 15:27).

b.   David offered priestly sacrifices before the Lord (II Samuel 6:17).

c.   David officiated in pronouncing the Aaronic priestly blessing upon the people in the name of the Lord (I Chronicles 16:1,2; Numbers 6:24-27).

d.   David set up another Tabernacle and placed the Ark of the Covenant of the Lord in it, even as Moses had set up his Tabernacle centuries before (I Chronicles 16:1; II Samuel 6:17).

e.   David's horn was to be like Aaron's priestly rod, and the Lord would cause it to bud; thus combining the King (horn) and Priest (rod) in the one person of David (Psalms 132:17; Numbers 17; Luke 1:69).

When king Saul and king Uzziah presumed into priestly ministrations, God judged them for seeking to combine the king-priestly ministry (I Samuel 15; II Chronicles 26). However, he did not judge David for this. David was an anointed king over the House of Judah and House of Israel. But he also touched something pertaining to priesthood, thus shadowing forth Jesus Christ, the Son of David, as King-Priest, after the Order of Melchisedek (I Samuel 16:1; II Samuel 2:4; 5:1-5). In these things David, though under the Aaronic Priesthood and Mosaic Covenant, shadowed forth the Melchisedek Priesthood under the New Covenant (Psalms 110; 133; Hebrews 7).

2.   The Levitical Priesthood

Though David left the majority of the Levitical priesthood to minister in the Tabernacle of Moses, according to the Mosaic Covenant, he appointed a great number of priests to minister in the Tabernacle of David according to the Davidic Covenant.

This company of priests were under the leadership of Chenaniah, the Master of Song, as well as Heman, Asaph and Ethan (I Chronicles 15:16-28; 16:1-6; 25:1-7). There were two companies of priests, performing two orders of worship, in two different sanctuaries, on two different mountains, according to two different covenants. The New Testament reveals that the Levitical priesthood was done away with and that the priesthood Order of Melchisedek was established. That which took place under the Davidic Covenant pointed to the ultimate fulfillment of the New Covenant (I Peter 2:5; Acts 6:7; Revelation 1:6; 5:9-10).

C.   The Sanctuary of the Covenant

Though David maintained the order of service in the Tabernacle of Moses, he was led by God to establish a Tabernacle on Mt Zion. There he brought the Ark of the Covenant which Eli's sons of the Aaronic order had removed from the Tabernacle at Shiloh and had lost in battle to the Philistines. He placed it in the tent he had pitched for it in Zion (I Chronicles 13; 15; 16; II Samuel 6:12-17; Acts 7:46; Isaiah 16:5; Amos 9:11; Acts 15:16).

The order of service of the Tabernacle of Moses was characterized by continual animal sacrifices and holy place ministrations without the Ark of God. The order of the Tabernacle of David was characterized by continual sacrifices of singing of praise with instruments of worship before the Ark of the Lord. It was this place of worship in Zion which God chose for His eternal habitation (Psalms 132).

From this point on in Scripture Zion carried a twofold significance commensurate with the ministry of David.

1. Zion—The City of David—The Political Centre

Zion became the capital city, the governing city of the nation and the city of the throne of king David. Here many of the kingly Zion Psalms were born (Psalms 48; 72; 110).

Earthly Zion foreshadowed heavenly Zion from which king Jesus rules and reigns over His people, the Church (Hebrews 12:22-24; Revelation 14:1-4; Psalms 2:6,7; Acts 4:23-36; Psalms 146:10).

2. Zion—The Tabernacle of David—The Religious Centre

Zion was also a sacred city, the religious capital of the nation. Here the Tabernacle of David order of worship was centered. Here the people of Israel gathered to worship and praise the Lord. Many Zion Psalms of worship were born here and testify of this fact (Psalms 9:11; 48:2, 11; 50:2). Zion with its throne and tabernacle involved both King and Priest together and pointed to the New Covenant order of Melchisedek. Here spiritual sacrifices of praise, worship and thanksgiving were offered (Psalms 65:1; 87:1-6; 99:1-2; 102:13-21; 134:3).

The fulfillment of the Tabernacle of David is found in Christ and the Church. Both Old Testament and New Testament show that Christ would sit in the Tabernacle of David, His Church, and that both Jew and Gentile would gather together to worship Him who is the greater Son of David (Isaiah 16:5; Amos 9:11,12; Acts 15:15-18). The writer to the Hebrews reveals that, after the cross, the believer is no longer under the Tabernacle of Moses of Sinai or the Mosaic Covenant with its Aaronic priesthood and animal sacrifices, but is under the Tabernacle of David of Zion and the New Covenant with its Melchisedek priesthood and spiritual sacrifices being offered to God through Christ (Hebrews 5-12).

That which David and the Levites experienced in the sacrifices, priesthood and tabernacle under the Davidic Covenant was consummated in Christ and the Church in the sacrifices, priesthood and tabernacle of the New Covenant.

III. The SEAL of the Covenant

Each of the Covenants had their particular sign and seal. Three Covenants refer in some way to the heavenly celestial bodies.

In the Noahic Covenant God used the rainbow as the token and seal. In the Abrahamic Covenant God used the multiplicity of the stars as a witness of the promise of multiplicity of Abraham's seed. But in the Davidic Covenant God used the heavenly bodies of the sun, moon and stars to be its sign and seal (Psalms 89:34-37; Jeremiah 32:35).

The sun, moon and stars were to be for signs, seasons, days and years (Genesis 1:14-19). God promised David that as long as the ordinances of heaven remained, the sun to govern the day and the moon and stars to govern the night, that David would have a seed upon his throne (Jeremiah 32:35-37; 33:19-26). Therefore, because these heavenly signs are still functioning, the throne of David continues to exist.

The ultimate fulfillment of the seal of the Davidic Covenant is found in Jesus Christ, who is the King of kings and Lord of lords, ruling and reigning over the redeemed, the spiritual Israel of God. This reign is in the eternal city of God that has no need of the light of the sun or the moon, for the Lord God and the Lamb are the light and glory thereof (Revelation 19:16; 21:1-27; 22:1-5).

SUMMARY

Christ Himself is the ultimate fulfillment of the Davidic Covenant. In Him David finds both his Lord (as to His Divinity) and his Son (as to His Humanity). He will return the second time without sin unto salvation and reign over all His redeemed Israel, both of the Old Testament and the New Testament, as King of kings and Lord of lords. The Kingdom shall be His and of the increase of His government and peace there shall be no end. He shall order it and establish because the zeal of the Lord of Hosts has spoken it and will perform it (Isaiah 9:6-9).

Chapter 9

THE NEW COVENANT

> The New Covenant was made by the Lord Jesus Christ immediately prior to His death at Jerusalem. It was made with the twelve apostles, who represented the House of Israel and the House of Judah, after the flesh, but were the foundation of the New Covenant Church, being the twelve apostles of the Lamb. It became the fulfilment of all previous Covenants, fulfilling and abolishing in itself their temporal elements and making possible their everlasting elements. The New Covenant makes possible and brings the believer into the Everlasting Covenant, thus completing the cycle of Covenantal revelation.

INTRODUCTION

The cycle of Covenant, Probation, Failure and Judgment certainly completes itself in relation to the chosen nation, and more especially the House of Judah, although representatively the House of Israel is included, at the first coming of the Lord Jesus Christ.

The chosen nation of Israel was a nation "to whom pertaineth the adoption, and the glory, and the *covenants,* and the giving of the law, and the service of God, and the promises; whose are the fathers and of whom as concerning the flesh Christ came, who is over all, God blessed for ever" (Romans 9:4,5).

The Edenic Covenant had been made with Adam before the entrance of sin. The Adamic Covenant was made after sin involving redemption for Adam's race. The Noahic Covenant had been made with the whole of mankind and all creatures. But all succeeding covenants had been made virtually with the chosen nation, Israel. It began with the Abrahamic Covenant, then progressed through the Mosaic, the Palestinian, and the Davidic Covenants. Covenantal revelation would consummate in the making of the New Covenant by their promised Messiah.

However, the tragic history of the nation shows repeated failure and judgment in spite of God's covenantal grace to the people of His choice. The Lord Jesus Christ came, born of a virgin, as the seed of the woman, the seed of Abraham, Isaac, Jacob and the seed of the house of David. He came to bring redemption from sin to them, as well as all other nations. He came to reveal God the Father to them. He came as the fulfilment and the fulfiller of all the covenantal promises given to their fathers (Romans 15:8). By the time Christ came the leaders of the Jewish nation had perverted and twisted the Mosaic Covenant by their traditions (Mark 7:1-15). They had become spiritually proud of their choice under the Abrahamic Covenant. They were characterised by hypocrisy, arrogance and lack of any spiritual perception.

Thus after 3½ years of miraculous ministry in word and deed, confirming the covenants of redemption, Jewry, as a whole, rejected the Christ of God. The Jewish Sanhedrin condemned Jesus to be crucified, and under Roman authority put Him to death. The nation filled up their cup of iniquity (Matthew 23:32). The crucifixion was the final act of transgression. Even after the Lord Jesus had made the New Covenant with the twelve apostles, had died, been resurrected and had poured out the Holy Spirit, grace was extended to Israel for another 40 years. But in 70 A.D. the period of probation for the nation came to an end. God allowed Prince Titus and the Roman armies to conquer the city of Jerusalem, destroy the Temple, and scatter Jewry from the land of Palestine. They became a people under covenant judgment and the curse of innocent blood.

There is no hope for Israel outside of Christ and New Covenant relationship with God through Him. The New Covenant is the last covenant ever to be made with the House of Israel and the House of Judah (Jeremiah 31:31-34). To have been the recipients of previous covenants, and to reject the New Covenant of God in Christ is to be placed outside of covenant promises and blessings for all eternity.

When it comes to the revelation of the New Covenant we discover that both God's foreknowledge and foreordained purpose are illustrated by the types and prophecies found under the Old Testament.

1.   **The New Covenant Typified**

Among the many types of the New Covenant found under the Old Testament the following stand out as major ones.

a.   **In Abraham's Two Sons**

In Galatians 4:21-31 Paul used the two sons of Abraham as an allegory to explain their representation of two covenants. Ishmael (Genesis 16) represented the Mosaic Covenant of law and works. Isaac (Genesis 21,22) represented the New Covenant of grace and faith. When Isaac was weaned it became apparent that Ishmael could not be the heir of the Abrahamic Covenant (Genesis 21). This foreshadowed that the Mosaic Covenant would be fulfilled and abolished when the New Covenant was ratified (Hebrews 10:9,16,17).

b.   **In Moses' Law**

In II Corinthians 3, Paul illustrated how the Mosaic Covenant was typical of the New Covenant. The words of the Old Covenant were written in two tables of stone, and though glorious, they were to be done away with. This pointed to the words of the New Covenant which are written on the two tables of the heart and mind. These are more glorious and are to last forever (Exodus 20; 31:18; Hebrews 8:6-13; 10:16,17).

c.   **In Marriage Laws**

In Romans 7:1-4 Paul illustrated how the Old Covenant marriage laws typified the transfer from the Mosaic Covenant to the New Covenant. Israel was married at Mt Sinai on the basis of the Mosaic Covenant. This marriage ended in divorce by reason of adultery (Jeremiah 3:1-14; 31:31-34; Isaiah 50:1). Because of the death and resurrection involved in the New Covenant Israel may now be joined to Christ in a new marriage.

d.   **In Circumcision**

In Romans 4 Paul refered to Abraham's being justified by faith, while un-circumcised, as an example of the Gentiles, the Uncircumcision, being justified by faith under the New Covenant. He also refered to the Jews, who were the Circumcision, under the Mosaic Covenant, as being justified by faith also under the New Covenant. Therefore, by reason of the New Covenant, Abraham is the father of all who believe, whether Jew or Gentile, Circumcision or Uncircumcision.

Now the true Jew is one who has experienced the spiritual circumcision of the heart, whether he be Jew or Gentile (Romans 2:24-29; Philippians 3:3).

2. **The New Covenant Prophesied**

Not only was the New Covenant typified in the Old Testament era, it was also clearly prophesied. Though the prophets of Israel and Judah were under the Mosaic Covenant they were able to prophesy of the New Covenant.

a. **By Isaiah**

Isaiah foretold the coming of the Redeemer to Zion and the turning from transgression by reason of the words and spirit of the coming New Covenant (Isaiah 59:20,21; Isaiah 61:8). That this was prophetic of the New Covenant is confirmed by the apostle Paul in Romans 11:26,27.

b. **By Jeremiah**

The prophet Jeremiah gave the clearest and fullest prophecy concerning the New Covenant that the Lord said He would make with the House of Judah and the House of Israel in the last days (Jeremiah 31:31-34; Hebrews 8; Jeremiah 32:38-40). It is this utterance that was dealt with by the writer to the Hebrews. He clearly stated how the Mosaic Covenant had become old, decayed and was ready to vanish away once the New Covenant was established (Hebrews 8:6-13; 10:16,17,29; 12:24; 13:20). Its promises involved a new heart and a new mind upon which the laws of God would be written instead of upon tables of stone.

c. **By Ezekiel**

Ezekiel also foretold the coming of the New Covenant (Ezekiel 16:60-62). Even though these prophets of Israel were under the Mosaic Covenant they prophesied of the New Covenant, which would be a better covenant. Ezekiel spoke of the fact that this covenant would be a covenant of peace (Ezekiel 34:25). It would involve cleansing by water, the reception of a new heart and a new spirit by the power of the Holy Spirit's work and the removal of the stony heart. These things are New Covenant promises (Ezekiel 11:16-21; 20:37; 37:25-27).

d. **By Hosea**

The prophet Hosea foretold the coming of the New Covenant both by his utterances and the symbolic marriage he experienced. Hosea found that his wife, the mother of his children, had played the harlot. Under God's instruction he put her away. The children born of Gomer had symbolic names: "Lo ru-hamah" meaning "Not having obtained mercy" and "Lo-ammi", "Not My people, and I will not be your God" (Hosea 1:6-9; 2:1-2).

All of this was symbolic of Jehovah's marriage to Israel. Because of Israel's national adultery, He gave her a bill of divorce (Jeremiah 3:1-14; Isaiah 50:1). He cast her off and thus they did not obtain mercy, they were not His people, and He was not their God under the Old Covenant economy.

However, God also spoke through Hosea saying that the people, though cast off, would be as the sand of the sea (an Abrahamic Covenant promise), and in due time would become the sons of the living God (a New Covenant promise). Hosea 1:10,11.

To illustrate this, God told Hosea to redeem Gomer back to himself. This he did and it became symbolic of the fact that though national Israel was divorced under the Old Covenant, by redemption under the New Covenant, at the cross, they could be restored back to God in covenantal relationship.

The New Testament writers, especially Paul and Peter, took these utterances of Hosea and used them to show that under the Old Covenant both Israel and the Gentiles found no mercy, and were not the people of God. But now, under the New Covenant, in Christ, they find mercy and become His people and He becomes their God (Romans 9:24-33; 11:26-32; I Peter 2:9,10).

3. **The New Covenant Personified**

Because all previous covenants pointed to and were to be fulfilled in Jesus Christ, the prophets also stated that the Lord Jesus Christ is the New Covenant personified.

He is the SEED of the Adamic, Noahic, Abrahamic, Mosaic and Davidic Covenants. The Father God, by the Spirit, spoke through the prophet Isaiah concerning the Messiah, His Son, saying: "I will give THEE for a covenant of the people" (Isaiah 42:6,7; 49:5-8 with II Corinthians 6:2).

The prophet Malachi speaks of the Lord Jesus as being "the Messenger of the covenant" (Malachi 3:1).

Seeing that the Lord Jesus Christ Himself is the New Covenant personified, two major facts should be considered relative to all other covenants.

a. **Temporal Elements Fulfilled and Abolished**

As previously noted, previous covenants had both temporal and everlasting elements. Jesus Christ, by the New Covenant, came to be the fulfilment of the Messianic promises in those covenants and by the cross abolish the temporal elements in those covenants. This may be illustrated by these examples.

* Christ is the Seed of the Adamic, Abrahamic, as well as the Noahic Covenant. As such He is the fulfilment of the "seed promises".

* The seal of the Abrahamic Covenant was circumcision, but, the sacramental value of this physical seal was abolished by the cross. It was replaced by circumcision of the heart and spirit; an internal rather than external seal. This temporal element of the Abrahamic Covenant was fulfilled and abolished (Matthew 1:1; Romans 2:25-29; Colossians 2:11,12).

* The Mosaic Covenant had numerous temporal elements; its laws on tables of stone, ceremonial sacrifices, priesthood, festival and sanctuary services. All of this was fulfilled and abolished at the cross by Christ. It was done away by fulfilment (II Corinthians 3; Hebrews 8-10).

b. **Everlasting Elements Remain**

Previous covenants had everlasting elements in them also. While the New Covenant fulfilled and abolished the temporal elements, it made possible the everlasting elements in these same covenants.

Things can only be eternal or everlasting by reason of Him who lives in the power of an endless life, and gives everlasting life to all who believe on Him (Hebrews 7:16; John 3:16).

Thus the "everlasting inheritance" of the Abrahamic Covenant, the "everlasting priesthood" of the Mosaic Covenant and the "everlasting throne and kingdom" of the Davidic Covenant can only be possible in and through Christ. It is the everlasting New Covenant, which is primarily spiritual and eternal in its elements that makes possible all the everlasting elements in former covenants.

I. The WORDS of the Covenant

When considering the words of the New Covenant it is necessary to begin with all the words of Jesus spoken in the Gospels. Then we may add to these the truths built on them in the Acts, the Epistles and Revelation. The words and blessings of the New Covenant, though voluminous, may be condensed in the following outline.

A. The Promises of the Covenant

Though not always stated in form of a promise the words of Jesus are indeed New Covenant promised blessings. Jesus Christ was made a minister of the circumcision "to *confirm the promises* made unto the fathers" (Romans 15:8).

New Covenant blessings are also the fulfilment of the previous covenants and their promised blessings. In Abraham's seed all nations were to be blessed. This finds its fulfilment in New Covenant blessing (Genesis 12:3; Galatians 3:8). The preaching, teaching, saving and healing ministry of Jesus Christ was all a confirmation of the covenants made with Adam, Abraham, Noah, Israel and David. All were intended to restore man back to the blessing and purpose God intended in the Edenic Covenant. However, the blessings of the New Covenant go far beyond those of Old Testament covenants.

1. Promises of Blessing

a. Blessing of Salvation

The word "salvation" includes in its meaning "safety, security, preservation, deliverance and wholeness".

The chief blessing of the New Covenant is the salvation of the soul. It is the greatest "spiritual blessing" (Ephesians 1:1-3) that Christ came to bring. Jesus Christ is the Saviour of the world (John 4:42; Acts 13:23). Theologically this "so great salvation" includes the following benefits, all made possible by the New Covenant in Christ (Hebrews 2:3).

(1) **Pardon** — the forgiveness and remission of the penalty of sin (Acts 10:43; 13:36-39). Jesus forgave sins (Luke 7:36-50; Matthew 9:2; Mark 2:5) and brought salvation to sinners (Luke 19:1-10). The Old Covenant simply covered forgiven sin while the New Covenant provides cleansing of forgiven sin (I John 1:5-9).

(2) **Justification** — the pronouncing just, a declaration of righteousness and right standing before God through Christ (Romans 5:1; 3:24-26). By the works of the Law, the Mosaic Covenant, none could be justified (Romans 3:19,20; Acts 15:8-11). The New Covenant makes possible justification by faith in an accomplished work.

(3) **Regeneration** — by which one is born again into the family of God and can call God "Father" (John 3:1-5; Matthew 6:9; I Peter 1:23). Under the Old Covenant none could be born again, but the New Covenant makes possible the miracle of the new birth.

(4) **Assurance** — whereby one has the witness of the Spirit that he is secure in obedience to the Word of God (Hebrews 5:8,9; 6:10-12; 10:38,39; I John 3:19). The Old Covenant believers never had the blessed assurance that New Covenant believers are given.

(5) **Sanctification** — whereby one is set apart unto the Lord and His holy service and use (John 17:17; I Thessalonians 5:23,24; Ephesians 5:26,27). The Old Covenant believers generally did not experience the blessing of sanctification made available for every believer under the New Covenant.

(6) **Adoption** — whereby one is placed as a son in the family of God (Romans 8:15,23; Galatians 4:5; Ephesians 1:13,14). By this act we are set in as mature members of the family of God and Jesus is the Firstborn among a vast family of brethren (Matthew 11:46-50; Romans 8:29). The Old Covenant believers never experienced this sonship as do New Covenant believers.

(7) **Glorification** — to render or esteem glorious, honorable, or to magnify. Glorification is the final work of redemption in the perfected saints. Man fell from the glory of God when he sinned under the Edenic Covenant (Romans 3:23). The New Covenant makes provision for the believer from justification to glorification (Romans 8:17,30). Old Covenant saints saw and experienced in small measure the glory of God, His majesty and brightness. The New Covenant brings the believer into the fulness of the glory of God (John 17:22-24; II Corinthians 3:18).

Though saints under previous covenants may have experienced some of these blessings in measure there is a uniqueness to these blessings because of New Covenant believer's experience of being "in Christ" by the miracle of the new birth. Those under the Adamic, Noahic, Abrahamic, and Davidic Covenants certainly knew pardon and justification by faith, all in anticipation of that which would come under the New Covenant (Hebrews 11; Romans 4). There were those even under the Mosaic Covenant who experienced pardon, justification and sanctification by faith in the coming New Covenant. However, the New Covenant sacrifice of Christ would make available redemption and salvation for all believers whether they were under the Old Testament or the New Testament (Hebrews 9:6-15). Such salvation and righteousness had been prophesied by the Old Testament prophets (Isaiah 51:1; 4-8; 53:11,12; Jeremiah 23:5,6; 33:15,16).

b. **Blessing of the Gospel of the Kingdom**

Christ not only came to bring salvation, but also to bring the good news of the kingdom of God. This involved the preaching and teaching ministry of Christ. The preaching and teaching of Jesus was an integral part of the words of the New Covenant, the Gospel of the Kingdom (Matthew 4:23-25; 9:35; 10:1-42; 24:14).

The Church is to be the instrument to continue the work that Jesus began to do and teach (Acts 1:1; Matthew 16:15-20). The Gospel of the Kingdom has to be preached to all the world for a witness to all nations before the end comes (Matthew 24:14; Matthew 28:18-20).

The Church in the Book of Acts preached and demonstrated that kingdom (Acts 1:3,6; 8:1,12; 19:8; 20:17-27; 28:23,31). By the preaching and reception of the Gospel people are born into the kingdom of God (John 3:1-5) and added to His Church (Acts 2:41-47; 5:14; 11:24). They are translated from the kingdom of darkness, given citizenship in the heavenly kingdom and seated with Christ on the throne of the kingdom (Colossians 1:13,14; Ephesians 2:5-19).

The teaching and preaching of Jesus covers all the basic laws and principles of kingdom living for New Covenant believers. Though these words are found in the Gospels as a whole, the major truths are especially in Matthew's didactic Gospel and these may be grouped in the following manner.

(1) The New Birth into the Kingdom — John 3:1-21.

(2) The Beatitudes — Matthew 5:1-12.

(3) The Laws of the Kingdom — Matthew 5:13-48; Luke 6:20-49.

(4) The Principles of Kingdom Living — Matthew 6-7.

(5) The Parables of the Kingdom — Matthew 13,20,21,22,25; Mark 4,8; Luke 15,19,20.

(6) Heart Condition — Matthew 11:1-30; 12:31-50; Matthew 15:10-20; Mark 7:14-23.

(7) Principles of the Ministry — Matthew 10; Luke 10.

(8) Traditions versus the Word of God — Matthew 15:1-9; Mark 7:1-13.

(9) The Bread of Heaven — John 6; Matthew 16:1-12.

(10) The Church and the Keys of the Kingdom — Matthew 16:15-28; 24:14.

(11) Concerning Offences and Forgiveness — Matthew 18; Mark 9; Luke 17:1-6.

(12) Concerning Divorce and Marriage and Children — Matthew 19:1-5; Mark 10:1-16.

(13) Concerning Riches and Stewardship — Matthew 19:16-30; Luke 12; 16:1-12.

(14) Having a Servant spirit — Matthew 20:17-28; Mark 10:32-45.

(15) The Cost of Discipleship — Luke 14.

(16) Concerning Taxes — Matthew 17:24-27; 22:15-22.

(17) Concerning Hell — Luke 16:19-31.

(18) Concerning Resurrection — Matthew 22:23-33; John 5.

(19) The Two Great Commandments of Love — Matthew 22:34-40.

(20) Concerning Hypocrisy — Matthew 23; Mark 11:37-54.

(21) Concerning Worship — John 4.

(22) Concerning True Judgment — John 8:1-11.

(23) Concerning the Father God — John 8:12-59.

(24) Concerning True Shepherds — John 10.

(25) Concerning Washing one another's feet — John 13.

(26) Concerning the Ministry of the Holy Spirit — John 14,15,16.

(27) Concerning Prayer for Unity among believers — John 17.

(28) Concerning Apocalyptic Events — Matthew 24; Mark 13; Luke 17:20-37; Luke 21.

(29) Concerning the Lord's Covenant Table — Matthew 26:17-30.

(30) Concerning the Great Commission to Evangelize — Matthew 28:16-20; Mark 16:15-20; Luke 24:49-53.

Things that are written in the Acts, the Epistles and Revelation are the words of Jesus given by the Holy Spirit through the apostles. All are amplification and application of the "seed-words" of Jesus. These are the New Covenant words. The Church is to preach, teach and live the laws and principles of the Gospel of the Kingdom.

c. **Blessing on the Gentiles**

The origin of the nations was seen in the Noahic Covenant. The blessing of all these nations was promised in the Abrahamic Covenant. But under the Mosaic Covenant the Gentile nations were excluded from blessing until the Messiah would come. In the beginning of His ministry Christ forbade His disciples to go to the Gentiles but rather to focus upon the lost sheep of the House of Israel (Matthew 10:1-8). This was to give the Jews the first opportunity to receive the Messiah. However, as the unbelief and hardness of the Jews' heart was exposed Christ began to minister to Gentiles, illustrating His intention to open the door of faith to the Gentiles in due time (John 1:11,12; Matthew 8:5-13; John 4:1-42; Matthew 15:21-28; Acts 14:27).

After His death and resurrection, but before His ascension, Christ commissioned His disciples to take the Gospel to all nations (Matthew 28:18-20; Mark 16:15-20; Acts 1:8; Galatians 3:8). This was to fulfill the mystery of the Gentiles coming into Messianic blessing and becoming one body in Christ with believing Jews. This mystery was predicted by the Old Testament prophets (Ephesians 2:11-22; 3:1-12; Romans 9-11; 15:8-16; Psalms 18:49; Deuteronomy 32:43; Psalms 117:1; Isaiah 11:1-10; 42:1-4; 52:13-15; 60:1-3; 65:1,2).

d. **Blessing of the Outpoured Spirit**

The Old Testament prophets spoke of the coming outpouring of the Spirit under Messiah's ministry and in New Covenant times (Joel 2:28-32; Isaiah 44:3; Ezekiel 36:25-27; Zechariah 12:10). These predictions were based on a covenant promise God had made to Abraham. The blessing that was to come upon all nations through Abraham's seed was "the promise of the Spirit" (Galatians 3:8,9,14,16,29).

Christ taught much concerning the coming of the Holy Spirit, the seal of the New Covenant (Luke 11:9-13; John 7:37-39; 14:16,17; 15:26; 16:7-15). The fulfilment of this promise began in the Book of Acts as both Jew and Gentile were baptized in the Holy Spirit (Acts 2,10,11).

e. **Blessing of Healing**

The prophets also foretold the Messiah's great healing ministry. Not only would He bring spiritual healing of the soul and spirit, but also physical healing of the body. Old Testament saints experienced touches of the healing power of the Lord at times. Israel had been given the covenant of healing from Jehovah Rapha, the Lord that heals (Job 42:10; Exodus 15:20-27; Psalms 105:37; II Chronicles 30:18-20). David spoke of the twin blessings of forgiveness of sin and healing of diseases (Psalms 103:1-4).

Prophet Isaiah foretold the fact that Messiah would take all our sickness and disease, as well as our sins, in His body on the tree and that by His stripes we would be healed (Isaiah 35; 53). The New Testament writers clearly interpret this to be speaking of the Messiah's healing ministry, spiritually, as well as physically (Matthew 8:16,17; I Peter 2:24). The Gospels abound with the healing ministry of Christ, which is a New Covenant blessing. Jesus, as the New Covenant personified, did the Father's will and confirmed the promises made to the fathers (Matthew 8,9,10; Luke 10:1-16; Romans 15:8).

Thus Christ, the Twelve apostles, the Seventy others and all believers could know the blessing of healing as a New Covenant promise. The healing ministry of Christ continues on in the Church (Mark 16:15-20; Acts 4; I Corinthians 12:1-12; James 5:14-16). Old Covenant saints never witnessed such healing power as did the generation that received the New Covenant Messiah's ministry.

f. **Blessing of Miracles**

In addition to spiritual and physical healing, the New Covenant Messiah blessed Jewry with great miracles: feeding the multitudes with bread and fish (Matthew 14,15); walking on the water (John 6:15-21); calming the troubled sea (Mark 4:36-41); water turned to wine (John 2), and many more miracles attested to the fact that Jesus was indeed confirming the covenant promise made to the fathers (John 20:30,31; Romans 15:8; Daniel 9:24-27).

Miracles took place under Christ's ministry that never took place under previous covenants. The gift of miracles has also been set in the Church to continue the New Covenant ministry of Christ (I Corinthians 12:1-13).

g. **Blessing of Deliverance**

One of the greatest blessings that the New Covenant Christ brought was deliverance from the power of Satan and from demonic possession, oppression and bondage. Jesus cast out the spirits with His word, and loosed people from Satanic power (Matthew 8:16,17; Mark 1:23-27,39; 5:1-20; Acts 10:38). All this was in fulfilment of that promise given in the Adamic Covenant, that the seed of the woman would bruise and crush the serpent's head (Genesis 3:15).

There is no record in the Old Testament era of any ministry having such power over Satan and his demonic forces. Such deliverance is part of the New Covenant blessings. The same ministry was given to the Twelve, the Seventy and the Church, Christ's Body (Luke 9:1-2; 10:1-20; Mark 16:15-20; Acts 16:16-18; Romans 16:20).

h. **Blessing of Resurrection**

When Adam and Eve broke the Edenic Covenant they came under the penalty of death, which was Satan's greatest power (Genesis 2:16; Hebrews 2:14,15). Old Testament saints looked forward to the breaking of the power of death (Psalms 16:9; 17:15; Isaiah 26:19; Job 19:25-27; Hosea 13:14; Daniel 12:1-3). There were even foreshadowings and examples of God's power over death being broken (Genesis 5:24; Hebrews 11:5; I Kings 17:17-24; II Kings 4:18-37; Jude 9). It was Christ, who both taught and demonstrated that He was the resurrection and the life, who conquered death for all mankind (John 5:28,29; 6:39-54; 11:25,26,43,44; Matthew 9:18-26; Luke 7:11-23). In defeating Satan, who had the power of death, Jesus obtained the keys of death and hell (Hebrews 2:14,15; Revelation 1:18). Man must experience spiritual resurrection from being dead in trespasses and sins to be able to experience the blessedness of the physical resurrection (John 5:24-29; Ephesians 2:1-4; Revelation 20:1-6; Acts 24:15; I Corinthians 15). God has given to the Church the power to at times raise people from the dead (Acts 9:36-42; 20:7-12).

i. **Blessing of Eternal Life**

In contrast to the fulness of death brought by sin, the greatest promise of the New Covenant is the fulness of eternal life brought by faith in the righteousness of Christ (John 3:16). This is to restore to man access to the tree of life which was taken from him under the Adamic Covenant after Adam had broken the Edenic Covenant (Genesis 2:17; Revelation 2:7; 22:2,14). This eternal life includes the sharing in God's life, relationship with Him, the quality of His Divine life and the duration of life everlasting (I John 5:11,12; John 5:39,40; Galatians 2:20; Hebrews 7:16).

2. **Promises of Cursing**

The curse was introduced when Adam fell from covenantal relationship in Eden's Paradise. The curse was laid on the serpent and on the earth to affect all mankind. The theme of the curse is seen also in the Noahic and Abrahamic Covenants. Under the Mosaic Covenant tremendous curses were pronounced upon the chosen nation, Israel, if they failed to keep the terms of the covenant. In the Palestinian Covenant the curse was laid on the promised land in judgment upon the disobedience of the people of God. However, the greatest curse ever to be uttered is that which is uttered by the Lord Jesus, the New Covenant Messiah (Hebrews 12:22-29). It is threefold in its aspect and is all-inclusive in its implication, touching both time and eternity.

a. **The Curse on the Jewish Nation**

Jesus came to His own people, the House of Judah, but His own received Him not (John 1:11). In spite of the fact that Jesus Christ was the fulfilment of the covenants given to them and that they witnessed the greatest ministry ever in the history of mankind, they crucified Him. In doing so they rejected Him who was the New Covenant personified. There is no other covenant to be made beyond the New Covenant. Their rejection resulted in a terrible curse being laid upon them by the Lord Jesus as well as by themselves.

This curse was symbolized by Jesus cursing the fig tree at the roots never to bear fruit again. Most expositors accept the fact that the fig tree was symbolic of the Jewish nation, who was fruitless, having nothing but the leaves of hypocritical religion (Mark 11:12-14,20-22; Jeremiah 24).

Also, when the Jews as a nation rejected Christ, they invoked upon themselves and their unborn generations the curse of innocent blood. The curse of innocent blood cannot be lifted until they accept that blood for cleansing (Matthew 27:24,25; Deuteronomy 19:10; Numbers 35:33,34).

b. The Curse of the Wicked Nations

Not only was the Jewish nation cursed for rejecting their Messiah, so all nations will be judged for rejecting Christ. Throughout their history, all nations have been judged for their idolatry and immorality (Romans 1:18-32; Isaiah 60:12; Jeremiah 18:9,10). This progression of judgment will culminate in the cursing of the nations in the Anti-Christal world system at the second coming of Christ (Daniel 2; 7; Revelation 18:1-5; Matthew 25:31-46).

c. The Eternal Curse

This curse of curses is executed at the Great White Throne judgment when all those who have rejected covenantal relationship with God will be banished to the lake of fire for eternal damnation (Revelation 14:9-11; 20:11-15; Matthew 25:41).

B. The Terms of the Covenant

As all covenants, whether revocable or irrevocable, have certain terms, so does the New Covenant. As a covenant of grace depending on faith above works it is greater than the Mosaic Covenant of law which depended on works above faith. God in His grace freely provided this New Covenant redemption, but grace did not exclude His setting forth of certain terms by which this redemption is received. Though this covenant is irrevocable it is not unconditional. Man must willingly receive what has been freely given (John 1:11-13).

1. Repentance

When Adam sinned he was rejecting and turning away from the covenant God had made with him. To restore covenantal relationship man must respond to God's covenantal initiative by turning from sin back to a posture of receiving and keeping God's covenant. This change of mind and turning to God is called repentance.

This first command of the Gospel is man's initial step back into covenantal relationship with God. Under the New Covenant man is called first to repent (Matthew 3:1-18; 4:17; Acts 2:37,38; 17:30; 26:20,21; Hebrews

6:1,21; Luke 24:49). Genuine repentance brought about by the Word and Spirit of God is evidenced by genuine sorrow and change. With faith, it results in the assurance of forgiveness of sins.

2. **Faith**

    Any covenant that is made requires trust and agreement with its words. The recipients of previous covenants were men of faith (Hebrews 11). Though in the New Covenant, repentance is the initial step, it is faith that becomes the channel through which the covenant benefits are received. Faith is the attitude in which the covenant must be held (Mark 1:15; Acts 20:21; Hebrews 11:6; Ephesians 2:8). In that Christ is the New Covenant personified, to be "in Christ" by believing in Him is to be in covenant with God (Acts 16:31; John 3:16,36; 6:47; Ephesians 1:1-4).

3. **Obedience**

    Faith is not only a passive attitude of trust in the person and words of the covenant, it also involves active obedience to the terms of the covenant (James 2:17-26; Hebrews 11:7,8). Jesus Himself said "If ye love Me, keep My commandments" (John 14:15; 15:10). In His teaching of the New Covenant, Jesus laid down many conditions. This is illustrated by how often He attached the word "if" to His covenantal promises (John 15:1-10; 7:37; Mark 11:22-26; Matthew 5,6,7). Through the New Covenant Jesus is "the author of eternal salvation to them that obey Him" (Hebrews 5:8,9).

    Though the believer of the New Covenant is not under the law of Moses, he is under the law of Christ (I Corinthians 9:20,21). The Old Covenant required *legal* obedience to its commandments but the New Covenant requires *loving* obedience to the commandments of Jesus (John 14:15; I John 3:22-24). The Old Covenant gave an external standard and required strict and full obedience to it before mercy was given. The New Covenant imparts an internal standard as well as the grace to be able to keep it (II Corinthians 3; Hebrews 8:6-13; Jeremiah 31:31-34).

    Jesus gave numerous commandments, some of which are listed here.

    a. The first commandment to love God (Matthew 22:37,38).
    b. The second commandment to love our neighbour (Matthew 22:39,40; John 13:34).
    c. The commandment of witness (Matthew 5:13-16).
    d. The commandment of righteousness (Matthew 5:17-20).
    e. The commandment of reconciliation (Matthew 5:21-26).
    f. The commandment concerning adultery and divorce (Matthew 5:27-32; 19:1-9).
    g. The commandment concerning oaths (Matthew 5:33-37).
    h. The commandment concerning retaliation (Matthew 5:38-42).
    i. The commandment concerning enemies (Matthew 5:43-47).
    j. The commandment concerning perfection (Matthew 5:48).
    k. The commandment concerning alms (Matthew 6:1-4).

l.   The commandment concerning prayer (Matthew 6:5-13).

m.   The commandment concerning forgiveness (Matthew 6:14,15; 18:21-35).

n.   The commandment concerning fasting (Matthew 6:16-18).

o.   The commandment concerning values (Matthew 6:19-34).

p.   The commandment concerning criticism (Matthew 7:1-5).

q.   The commandment concerning discretion (Matthew 7:6).

r.   The commandment concerning requests (Matthew 7:7-11).

s.   The commandment concerning consideration (Matthew 7:12).

t.   The commandment concerning self-discipline (Matthew 7:13,14).

u.   The commandment concerning character and ministry (Matthew 7:15-23).

v.   The commandment concerning obedience (Matthew 7:24-27).

w.   The commandment concerning communion (Matthew 26:26-29).

x.   The commandment concerning water baptism (Matthew 28:19,20).

y.   The commandment concerning the Gospel (Mark 16:15-18; Acts 1:8).

z.   The commandment concerning the Holy Spirit (Luke 24:49; Acts 1:4,5).

Jesus' commandments are summarized in the word "love" (Matthew 22:37-40; I John 5:3; II John 6; Romans 13:8-10). While salvation is by grace through faith, the New Covenant believer who loves Jesus will keep His commandments.

C.   **The Oath of the Covenant**

As the Noahic, Abrahamic and Davidic Covenants were confirmed with oaths, so also is the New Covenant. The oath of this covenant is particularly focused on the priesthood of Christ. Because the Abrahamic Covenant and Davidic Covenant were preparatory to the New Covenant, their King-Priesthood finds its fulfilment in Jesus. The Book of Hebrews substantiate that Christ's priesthood is after the order of Melchisedek in that He lives in the power of an endless life (Hebrews 7). Thus this oath of an unchangeable priesthood was given prophetically in the Old Testament and is fulfilled in the person of the Lord Jesus Christ. It is this eternal priesthood of Christ that fulfills and abolishes the Aaronic priesthood of the Mosaic Covenant and makes the New Covenant irrevocable.

D.   **The Book of the Covenant**

The 27 Books of the New Testament contain the elements of the New Covenant made by Christ. For simplification it may be set out in the following manner:

*   **The Gospels** — The *Words* and the *Sacrifice* of the Covenant.

*   **The Acts** — The *Sign* and *Seal* of the New Covenant.

*   **The Epistles** — The *Sanctuary* of the New Covenant.

*   **The Revelation** — The *Consummation* and *Realization* of the New Covenant.

II. **The BLOOD of the Covenant**

A. **The Sacrifice of the Covenant**

1. **The Fulfilment of Old Testament Sacrifices**

    The sacrifice of the New Covenant fulfills all previous covenantal sacrifices. It is not only the supreme sacrifice but it is also the only sacrifice that can thoroughly cleanse man from sin. All others merely pointed to and were anticipatory of this once-for-all sacrifice for sin (Hebrews 9,10).

2. **The Body and Blood of Jesus**

    A study of the Old Testament sacrificial system given to Israel illustrates how particular God was when it came to the details concerning the body and blood of the victims.

    *   The *body* of the Burnt Offering had to be wholly burnt on the altar; the *blood* had to be sprinkled according to God's command (Leviticus 1).

    *   Also the *body* and *blood* of the Sin and Trespass Offerings were dealt with in the God-ordained way (Leviticus 4,5). The same was true concerning the sacrifices on the Day of Atonement (Leviticus 16); the sacrifice of the red heifer (Numbers 19), and the festival sacrifices (Exodus 12; Numbers 28,29; Leviticus 23).

    All of this pointed to and finds its fulfilment in that which pertained to the *body* and *blood* of the New Covenant sacrifice of Jesus. The Old Testament covenantal sacrifices typified the perfect, once-for-all sacrifice of Jesus. All the sacrificial bodies and blood of previous covenants prophesied of Christ who is the New Covenant personified.

    The writer to the Hebrews devotes two chapters to the body and blood of Jesus in heaven for us. Hebrews 9 deals with the blood, while Hebrews 10 deals with the body; both chapters showing their supremacy over animal bodies and animal blood. Untold thousands of animal sacrifices were offered in Old Testament times under covenant, but Jesus offered one perfect, sinless, human sacrifice, once-for-all (Hebrews 10:11-14). The evidence of this sacrifice is in heaven. The body and blood of Jesus are incorruptible and therefore eternal. These will be the eternal evidences of our salvation, both having been supernaturally taken to heaven. Jesus, of the New Covenant, would not have entered heaven without blood, even as Aaron of the Old Covenant dare not enter the earthly sanctuary without blood (Hebrews 9:7). It is the blood which makes atonement for the soul (Leviticus 17:11-14). It is when God sees the blood of atonement that He accepts the believer (Exodus 12:12,13).

    The body and blood of Jesus did not perish at Jerusalem, nor did they see corruption. They are in heaven for us now and have been accepted of the Father as the basis of Christ's mediatorial and intercessory ministry. Following are some of the most outstanding truths concerning the New Covenant sacrifice, the holy body and holy blood of Jesus.

    a. **His Body**

        (1) His body in heaven is the result of the miraculous incarnation. It is His virgin born body, prepared of the Holy Spirit in the virgin

Mary on earth (Hebrews 10:5-8; Luke 1:30-33; Matthew 1:18-21).

(2) His body in heaven once experienced sinless infirmities, suffering and death, but now is resurrected, glorified and no longer subject to weariness, pain or death (John 19:34,35).

(3) His body in heaven is the surety of our entrance into heaven (Hebrews 7:22).

(4) His body in heaven will be the eternal evidence of His perfect sacrifice, for it still has the wounds, though glorified, in His hands, feet and side (John 20:24-29).

(5) His body in heaven is the guarantee that the bodies of the saints will be raised and glorified. His body is the sample, the firstfruits of the harvest of the resurrected and immortalized redeemed (I Corinthians 15:51-57; Philippians 3:21; I Thessalonians 4:15-18).

(6) His body originated on earth and was taken to heaven, thus transcending natural laws, moving in higher and spiritual laws. The saints also will have bodies like Christ's that are adapted to the celestial realms for all eternity (Philippians 3:21).

(7) His body once sacrificed for sins as the New Covenant sacrifice, forever fulfills and abolishes all previous covenant sacrifices. His sacrifice, as the Lamb of God, will be eternally fresh before the throne of God. The cross was "the altar" upon which Jesus was sacrificed (Revelation 5:6; John 1:29,36; I Peter 1:19,20; Daniel 9:24-27; Hebrews 10:1-3; Hebrews 13:10-13).

b. **His Blood**

The blood of Christ is the most holy and precious thing. It is the only cleansing agent for sin in the universe (I Peter 1:18-20). It is the blood of God (Acts 20:28). It is far more valuable than animal blood, sinful human blood, for it is the Divine life, the blood of God. It speaks to God on our behalf (Hebrews 12:22-24). All true believers have faith in the blood of Jesus that was shed on earth at Calvary 2000 years ago but is now in heaven for us.

Some of the benefits which the believer receives by reason of the New Covenant blood of Jesus being in heaven are noted here.

(1) Cleansing from sin by the blood (I John 1:7).

(2) Justification available by the blood (Romans 5:9).

(3) Redemption through the blood (Ephesians 1:7; Romans 5:9,10).

(4) Reconciliation through the blood (Colossians 1:20; Romans 3:25).

(5) Peace with God through the blood (Colossians 1:20).

(6) Access to God by the blood (Ephesians 2:13).

(7) Conscience purged through the blood (Hebrews 9:13).

(8) Sanctification by the blood (Hebrews 13:12).

(9) Communion through the blood (I Corinthians 10:16).

(10) Covenantal relationship through the blood (Hebrews 13:20).

(11) Kings and Priests unto God through the blood (Revelation 1:5; 5:9,10).

(12) Overcome Satan by the blood (Revelation 12:11).

(13) Eternal life through the blood (John 6:53-63).

(14) Perfection by the power of the blood (Hebrews 6:1-2; 7:11-19).

All that the believer receives from God through Christ is because of the New Covenant efficacious blood of Jesus which is in heaven before the Father's throne.

Theologically the sacrifice of Christ is spoken of as:

(a) An Atonement (Romans 5:11; John 1:29,36).

(b) A Propitiation (Romans 3:25; I John 2:2; 4:10).

(c) A Substitution (I Peter 3:18; Romans 5:8).

(d) A Redemption (Colossians 1:14).

(e) A Ransom (Mark 10:45; I Timothy 2:5,6).

(f) A Reconciliation (II Corinthians 5:18-21; Hebrews 2:17).

These words together constitute the full truth of the Atoning work of the Lord Jesus Christ. In the atonement the sinless Christ took our sins and iniquities and suffered the wrath of a righteous and holy God, receiving in Himself the penalty of sin which was death. His death was not an accident but an accomplishment. In contrast to all previous covenantal sacrifices, which were unwilling animals, Christ's New Covenant offering was of His own voluntary will (Psalms 40:6-8; Hebrews 10:1-10; John 5:3).

3. **The Table of the Lord**

The Lord Jesus, before His crucifixion, resurrection and ascension, established an ordinance by which the Church could remember Him and partake of the power and presence of His sacrifice. This ordinance is the Lord's Table, or the Communion (Matthew 26:26-28; Luke 22:19,20).

The bread broken symbolized His broken body. The outpoured wine symbolized His outpoured blood. Thus the bread and the wine became symbolic of the New Covenant sacrifice of Jesus. The table of the Lord is a covenant table. Paul received special insight into the New Covenant table and wrote to the believers at Corinth concerning the necessity of eating and drinking worthily of the body and blood of Christ, the covenantal sacrificial symbols (I Corinthians 11:23-34). Every time believers gather together at the table of the Lord, they are confessing their unity and covenant relationship with the Lord and with each other. Failure to properly discern the body of Christ is to betray each other. It causes division and violates the covenant. Instead of bringing covenantal blessing, it brings covenantal judgment.

The body and blood of Jesus in heaven makes real and meaningful, by the power and presence of the Holy Spirit in earth, the bread and the wine to the Church as each ones partakes in faith (John 6:53-63; Hebrews 9:17-23). The New Covenant table becomes our "altar" unto God for priestly communion, even as was the table of shewbread in the Old Covenant sanctuary (Hebrews 13:10-13; Exodus 25:23-30).

4. **Spiritual Sacrifices**

Christ has commissioned the Church to offer spiritual sacrifices to God, not to atone for sins but to exemplify the spirit of the atonement (I Peter 2:5-9; Psalms 50:5). The Church which Christ died for is to live out the implications of His death. some of these spiritual sacrifices are:

a. Sacrifice of righteousness (Psalms 4:5; 51:19).

b. Sacrifice of joy (Psalms 27:6).

c. Sacrifice of a broken and contrite spirit (Psalms 51:17).

d. Sacrifice of thanksgiving (Psalms 107:22; 116:17).

e. Sacrifice of our bodies as a living sacrifice (Romans 12:1,2).

f. Sacrifice of praise (Hebrews 13:15).

g. Sacrifice of good deeds (Hebrews 13:16).

h. Sacrifice of fellowship (Hebrews 13:16).

B. **The Mediator of the Covenant**

1. **The Fulfilment of All Priesthood**

Under previous covenants God had foreshadowed the coming priesthood of Christ under the New Covenant. Patriarchal, Aaronic, Levitical and Kingly-Priests all pointed to that which would be fulfilled in Christ and the Church. That which was temporal in these priesthoods was abolished at the cross while that which is eternal passed through the cross and finds fulfilment in the New Covenant order of Melchisedek.

2. **The Priesthood of Christ**

The priesthood of Christ as our New Covenant Mediator surpasses all that was typified in Old Covenant Mediators. Christ is the mediator of a better covenant, which is the New Covenant (Hebrews 8:6; 9:15; I Timothy 2:5,6; Hebrews 12:24).

The Epistle to the Hebrews especially sets forth the glories of Christ's priesthood in contrast to the mediatorial work and priesthood of Moses, Aaron and the Levites (Hebrews 5,6,7).

Following are the major reasons why Christ's New Covenant priesthood supercedes all previous covenantal priesthoods.

a. **He is a Sinless Priest** (Hebrews 5:1-5; 8:1-4; 10:1-11).

In contrast to Moses, Aaron and all other priests who needed redemption, Christ needed no redemption. He was a sinless High Priest and therefore far superior to any Old Covenant mediator. The New Testament writers jealously guarded the fact of Christ's sinlessness (II Corinthians 5:18-21).

b. **He is a Divine-Human Priest** (Hebrews 2:17; John 1:1-3,14-18; I Timothy 2:5).

Not only was Christ a sinless mediator, He was also a perfect mediator, as a Divine-human person. A mediator in the truest sense must be able to understand perfectly the parties which need reconciliation. He must be able to fully identify with both to effectively mediate between them. In other words, if Jesus Christ is to be a perfect mediator between a holy God and sinful man, He must have the nature of God and the nature of man (sin excepted) to fully understand both and to effect reconciliation between them. Moses and Aaron or any other covenant priests could never do this fully because they had only one nature, sinful human nature. No priest of the Old Testament could ever be a perfect mediator.

Jesus Christ was the God-Man. He was God, having the nature of God, thus identifying with God in His absolute holiness. He also became Man, taking sinless humanity upon Himself and thus identifying with man. It is this union of the Divine and Human natures in the one person of Christ which qualifies Him to be a perfect mediator between God and man. He is the answer to the cry of Job for a Daysman "to lay His hand upon us both" (Job 9:32,33; 16:21; 19:25,27; 23:3-10).

Because Christ is the New Covenant personified and because He is the God-Man by reason of the union of the Divine and Human natures in Him, He is able to be both offerer and offering, sacrifice and sacrificer, priest and gift, heavenly and earthly, spiritual and natural. In His deity, He is the offerer, the sacrificer, the priest. In His humanity, He is offering, sacrifice and gift (Ephesians 5:2,25; Hebrews 8:3; 10:1-14; Galatians 2:20; Titus 2:14; Hebrews 2:17).

On the cross it was the Divine nature offering the sinless human nature to God. It was deity presenting sinless humanity to God as a perfect sacrifice for sin. It was God atoning to God. It was a sinless Man atoning for sinful man. Only the miracle of the incarnation and the union of the two natures in the one person could make this possible. Therefore Jesus is both the New Covenant sacrifice (His human nature, His body and blood) and the New Covenant priest (His Divine nature).

c.   **He is a King-Priest**

His priesthood is after the Order of Melchisedek, that is, He is a King-Priest. Previous covenants generally had priests, but only a few persons touched in measure that which belongs to the Order of Melchisedek. Through Israel's history under the Mosaic Covenant, the Kingship was given to the tribe of Judah and the Priesthood was given to the tribe of Levi. Jesus Christ combines in Himself both offices of King and Priest. It is this that constitutes the New Covenant priesthood, as is noted in the following outline.

(1) **Christ as Priest**

(a) As Priest He speaks to God on behalf of man (Hebrews 5:1-10; 8:1).

(b) As Priest He was chosen from among men (Hebrews 5:1).

(c) As Priest He was appointed and anointed by God (Hebrews 5:4,10).

(d) As Priest He made the sacrifice for sin (Hebrews 5:1-5; 7:8-18; 8:1-5; Romans 3:25,26).

(e) As Priest He makes intercession (Hebrews 4:15; 7:25; 9:11-28; 10:19-22).

(f) As Priest He can be faithful to God, yet merciful to His people (Hebrews 5:1-6; 2:17,18).

(g) As Priest He can be the mediator between God and Man (I Timothy 2:5,6; Zechariah 6:12,13; I John 2:1,9).

(h) As our Great High Priest He can direct the Church as His priestly body in earth is the ministry of reconciliation (II Corinthians 5:19-21).

(i) As Priest He can direct and lead the worship of the believing covenant community to the Father (John 4:20-24; Revelation 5:1-10; Hebrews 2:12).

(2) **Christ as King**

(a) As King He sits enthroned with the Father God (Zechariah 6:12,13; Revelation 3:21; 22:1; Mark 16:15-20).

(b) As King He exercises authority over all things in heaven and earth (Matthew 28:18-20).

(c) As King all enemies are to be placed under His feet. He reigns until the last enemy, death, has been destroyed (I Corinthians 15:24-28).

(d) As King He rules and reigns in righteousness, peace and joy (Romans 14:7; Isaiah 32:1).

(e) As King all the kingdoms of this world are to be subjected to Him (Daniel 7:1-4; Psalms 22:28; 72:11; Revelation 11:15-19).

(f) As King He rules in the Church, His Body, which is also after the Order of Melchisedek, or order of kings and priests unto God (I Peter 2:5-9; Revelation 1:5,6; 5:9,10; 20:6; Ephesians 1:20-22).

Because Jesus offered a perfect covenant sacrifice, He has accomplished a finished work and has sat down in the throne of God as a King and Priest of the New Covenant. All previous sacrifices, priesthoods and covenants pointed to this fact. He began His atoning work on earth at the cross as sacrifice and priest, but continues His work in heaven at the throne of God as King and Priest. The cross is the basis for His ministry on the throne. His priesthood shows Him to be the perfect Mediator, Reconciler, Intercessor and Advocate for all saints, especially for New Covenant believers.

3. **The Priesthood of All Believers**

In that the Church is the Body of Christ, it is the visible manifestation and expression of Christ in the earth. Thus, the Church's ministry is an extension of His ministry. The Church is identified with Christ in His Melchisedek priesthood as kings and priests unto God (I Peter 2:5-9; Revelation 1:5,6; 5:9,10; 20:6). It is the Church, as a kingdom of priests, that fulfills the ministry offered to Israel at Mt Sinai but was rejected by them (Exodus 19:3-6). This ministry involves:

a. **Priestly Ministry**

    (1) Priestly Worship (Revelation 5:9,10).

    (2) Priestly Sacrifice (I Peter 2:5).

    (3) Priestly Intercession (I Timothy 2:1,2).

    (4) Priestly Reconciliation (II Corinthians 5:18-21).

b. **Kingly Ministry**

    (1) Kingly Authority (Luke 10:17-20).

    (2) Kingly Conquest (Romans 16:20).

    (3) Kingly Administration (Revelation 20:6).

    (4) Kingly Benevolence (Matthew 5:43-48).

C. The Sanctuary of the Covenant

1. The Fulfilment of Old Testament Sanctuaries

The previous covenants had earthly and material altars and sanctuaries. These were all patterned after the heavenly sanctuary and pointed to the fullest expression of God's sanctuary in the earth.

Just as Christ is the fulfilment of all Old Testament sacrifices and priesthoods, so He is the fulfilment of all Old Testament sanctuaries. By His incarnation He became the dwelling place of God (John 1:14; 2:18-21; II Corinthians 5:21; I Timothy 3:16; Colossians 1:19; 2:9). Since the cross and the abolition of material temples "made with hands", the Church, both individually and corporately, has become God's New Covenant temple (Acts 7:47-50; I Corinthians 3:16,17; 6:16; Ephesians 2:19-22; I Peter 2:5-9).

2. The Heavenly Sanctuary

Scripture clearly teaches the existence of a heavenly sanctuary (Revelation 11:15-19; 15:1-5). It was here that sin began when Satan and his angels rebelled (Isaiah 14:12-14; Ezekiel 28:11-19; John 8:44), making the heavens unclean in God's sight (Job 15:15). Christ left the heavenly sanctuary and by the incarnation took upon Himself body and blood. He made the supreme sacrifice for sin, whereby both the heavens and the earth would be cleansed from the power and presence of sin. The writer to the Hebrews declares that after His completed sacrifice on earth, Christ ascended back to the heavenly sanctuary from which He exercises His King-Priestly ministry (Hebrews 8,9).

3. The Lord Jesus Christ

Coming from the heavenly eternal sanctuary Christ fulfilled the earthly temporal sanctuaries in His own being. As the Word made flesh He became God's perfect tabernacle. The fulness of the Godhead dwelt in Him bodily (John 1:14; Colossians 1:19; 2:9). In Him God's name and Shekinah Glory were revealed (Acts 2:34-36; John 1:14-18; Matthew 17:1-5). He was God's earthly temple as well as God's eternal temple (John 2:18-21; Revelation 21:22).

4. **The Church**

Christ not only ministers in the heavenly sanctuary but also ministers in the Church, His earthly sanctuary (Revelation 1-2-3). Even under Old Testament times there was both the earthly and heavenly sanctuaries (I Kings 7,8). Since the ascension of Christ the Church has been God's earthly dwelling place replacing all previous earthly dwelling places and sanctuaries (Acts 7:46-50). God's name and glory are now revealed in the Church which is Christ's Body (Matthew 28:18-20; Acts 2:34-36; Ephesians 3:21; 1:19-23). It is the coming together of the members of the Body of Christ that constitutes the place of the New Covenant priesthood, sacrifice and sanctuary in earth (Matthew 18:20; Ephesians 2:19,20; Hebrews 10:25; I Peter 2:5-9; I Timothy 3:15,16).

III. **The SEAL of the New Covenant**

As the seals of previous covenants were given to be ongoing reminders of the authenticity and validity of the covenant, so God attached a seal to the New Covenant to do the same thing. In this respect each covenant had its own sign or seal and God never took the seal of one covenant and attached it to another. However, the seals of all previous covenants are fulfilled in the seal of the New Covenant. In the scope of the New Covenant, the temporal and earthly elements are swallowed up in its spiritual reality.

In the Gospels we find that Jesus Christ Himself, the New Covenant sacrifice and priest, spoke many covenant words concerning the coming of the Holy Spirit, for the Holy Spirit Himself is the seal of the New Covenant (John 14,15,16). The Holy Spirit is the New Covenant seal personified, as Jesus is the New Covenant words, sacrifice, priest and sanctuary personified.

The Holy Spirit is spoken of as:

*   The *Seal* of the Covenant (Ephesians 1:13,14; 4:20; II Corinthians 1:22).

*   He gives the *Sign* of the Covenant which was evidenced in the speaking with other tongues on the Day of Pentecost (Mark 16:15-20; Acts 2:1-4).

*   He is also the *Executor* of the covenant to see that the last will and testament of Jesus is carried out in the believer's life (John 14:26; 15:26).

It is His indwelling in the believer that makes possible the blessings of the covenant, that validates his faith in the covenant, that enables obedience to the covenant and makes him God's covenant sanctuary.

Though Old Testament saints were temporarily anointed and energized by the Spirit, it is only the New Covenant saints that experience His indwelling and abiding presence (Judges 6:34; 14:6; John 14:16,17; Romans 8:9; I Corinthians 3:16; I John 2:20,27).

In that Jesus is the mediator and personification of the New Covenant, He has received the Spirit without measure. He also has the prerogative to administer the Holy Spirit as the seal of the New Covenant (John 1:32,33; 3:33,34; Matthew 3:11; Acts 1:5; Luke 24:49; John 15:26). The New Covenant believer is to experience the *fulness* of the Holy Spirit's ministry.

Because the Holy Spirit Himself is the seal of the New Covenant and is the fulfilment of all previous signs and seals, we note in outline form His major operations in the New Covenant believer.

A.   The Holy Spirit brings the new birth (John 3:5,6; Titus 3:5).

B.   The Holy Spirit indwells the believer's spirit (Romans 8:9; John 14:16,17; I Corinthians 3:16; 6:17; I John 2:27).

C.   The Holy Spirit is the anointing who abides within and teaches the New Covenant believer (I John 2:20,27; John 16:13).

D.   The Holy Spirit gives assurance of salvation (Romans 8:16).

E.   The Holy Spirit fills the believer with Himself (Acts 2:4; Ephesians 5:18).

F.   The Holy Spirit by the baptism in the Spirit enables the New Covenant believer to speak in unknown languages and edify himself (Acts 2:4; 10:44-46; Mark 16:17; I Corinthians 14:2,4,18).

G.   The Holy Spirit enables the believer to pray (Jude 20; Romans 8:26-28).

H.   The Holy Spirit enables the New Covenant believer to worship in spirit and in truth (John 4:23,24; Philippians 3:3; I Corinthians 14:15).

I.   The Holy Spirit leads and guides the believer into all truth (John 16:13; Romans 8:14).

J.   The Holy Spirit enables the believer to put to death the deeds of the flesh (Romans 8:13).

K.   The Holy Spirit produces the Christ-like nature and character in the life of the believer (Galatians 5:22,23; II Peter 1:4).

L.   The Holy Spirit empowers the New Covenant believer to be a witness for Christ (Acts 1:8; Isaiah 61:1; Luke 24:49).

M.   The Holy Spirit gives spiritual gifts to those whom He fills (I Corinthians 12:7-13).

N.   The Holy Spirit will bring about the resurrection and immortality of the believer's body in the last day. Such will consummate the Spirit's work as the seal of God (Romans 8:11; I Corinthians 15:47-51; I Thessalonians 4:15-18).

The acceptance of the New Covenant words, promises, sacrifice and priesthood in Christ Himself makes it possible for the New Covenant believer to receive the Holy Spirit Himself, as the New Covenant seal. The seal of the New Covenant is a person, the blessed Spirit Himself.

The operations of the Spirit are spoken of as:

*   The Seal (Ephesians 1:13,14; 4:30);

*   The Earnest (II Corinthians 1:22; 5:5; Ephesians 1:13,14);

*   The Firstfruits (Romans 8:23).

These operations point to the fact that the fulness and consummation of such operations, made possible by the New Covenant, will bring us into that which was planned by God in the Everlasting Covenant (Hebrews 13:20).

SUMMARY

In contrast to previous covenants with their animal sacrifices and impersonal seals, the New Covenant distinctly involves each of the persons in the Godhead.

* **The Father** — The Words of the Covenant spoken by Jesus were the Father's words (John 12:44-50; 8:38).

* **The Son** — The Body and Blood of Jesus were the Sacrifice of the Covenant, and He is also the Priest (Hebrews 10:5-10,29; 12:24; 13:20).

* **The Holy Spirit** — The Seal of the New Covenant is the Holy Spirit (Ephesians 1:13,14; 4:20; II Corinthians 1:22).

Chapter 10

THE EVERLASTING COVENANT

> The Everlasting Covenant is that Covenant made in Eternity, before Time began, in the counsels of the eternal Godhead, between the Father, Son and Holy Spirit. It was made before the creation of man and the entrance of sin into the human race. It embodies, as an all-encompassing Covenant, God's complete plan involving Creation and Redemption. It is the heavenly foundational Covenant in eternity for all Covenants revealed in Time. Man was not a party to it but the object of it.

INTRODUCTION

The Scripture clearly teaches that God had an *"eternal purpose"* before Time began and before the creation of man and the entrance of sin into the human race by the Fall of Adam and his wife. This "eternal purpose" was contained in the form of the Everlasting Covenant, for God declares no purpose apart from Covenant. This overriding purpose of the Everlasting Covenant provided the basis for the purposes revealed in the covenants made on earth in Time (Ephesians 3:11; Romans 8:27-30; Ephesians 1:9; Hebrews 13:20).

Of the eight Divine Covenants revealed in time, these being the Edenic, Adamic, Noahic, Abrahamic, Mosaic, Palestinian, Davidic and New Covenants, the first pertains to God's purpose in creation, while the next six are covenants of promise promising and symbolizing redemption before the cross, while the remaining or eighth covenant pertains to God's realized redemptive purposes in Christ Jesus.

As seen in the Edenic Covenant, God had a purpose for Adam and his offspring. This Covenant involving God's purpose for man was made *before* the entrance of sin. There we see the covenant cycle begin. Man is put on a period of probation, which ends in failure and judgment. Then God initiates the first link in the chain of the Covenants of redemption, the Adamic Covenant.

As tragic as the entrance of sin was into the human race, it should be recognized that God was not caught unawares. Because of His essential attributes He foresaw the fall of man from His creative purposes. Thus He set in motion the Covenants of redemption to redeem man from sin. The culminating New Covenant actually becomes the covenant of redemption by which God restores man back to His original purpose in the Edenic Covenant of creation. The New Covenant makes the Edenic Covenant possible. However, it was the pre-existent Everlasting Covenant in heaven that made possible all the Covenants of Creation and Redemption on earth. The Everlasting Covenant, as unfolded in creation and redemption could only be realized because of God's essential and moral attributes (Hebrews 13:20). Therefore the Everlasting Covenant is:—

1. **Possible because of God's Essential Attributes**

    a. **God is Eternal** — that is, He inhabits eternity, hence He could and did plan things in eternity (Isaiah 57:15; Genesis 21:33; Deuteronomy 33:27; Psalms 41:13; 90:2; 93:2).

b. **God is Omniscient** — He is all-knowing and knew before the creation of man as a freewill being that he would choose the tree of the knowledge of good and evil. Because of His omniscience He purposed to redeem all men who would come to Him on His terms (Acts 15:18). Omniscience includes wisdom, knowledge and understanding required to carry out covenantal purposes.

c. **God is Omnipotent** — He is all-powerful. Because of this His power can be operative both in creation and redemption. His sovereignty over creation and creatures is evident (Daniel 7:17).

d. **God is Omnipresent** — He is everywhere present at all times. No person can hide from His presence and the convicting power of the Holy Spirit (Psalms 139:7-12).

e. **God is Immutable** — He is unchanging as to His nature, being and character and covenant purposes (Malachi 3:6; Hebrews 13:8).

f. **God is Self-Existent** — He exists in and of Himself and is independant of time, space and all creatures. He is the Life-source and can act out of this eternal life accordingly and give life to all creatures (John 1:1-4; 3:16).

If it were not for these essential attributes of God, no covenant could have been made in eternity and certainly none could have been made and fulfilled in time.

2. **Available because of God's Moral Attributes**

a. **God is Holy** — He is absolute holiness and purity and cannot tolerate sin (Leviticus 19:2; 11:44,45; I Peter 1:16).

b. **God is Righteous** — He is perfectly just and must judge sin. Righteousness is the holiness of God in judgment upon man's sinfulness (Psalms 119:142; Deuteronomy 32:4; Romans 1:17).

c. **God is Love** — He is perfect love, grace, mercy and kindness manifested towards His creatures. Love was the Divine motive in the covenant of creation, and love was the motivation in the Covenants of redemption (I John 4:8,16; John 3:16; 14:23; Galatians 2:20).

d. **God is Faithful** — He is absolutely reliable, dependable and will be stedfastly committed to His covenant words and obligations to the man He created (Psalms 119:144; Hebrews 6:12-20; II Timothy 2:13; I Peter 4:19).

3. **Eternal because of the Eternal Godhead**

The "everlasting covenant" is an eternal covenant because it is not a covenant between God and man, though it involves man. It is a covenant between the persons of the eternal Godhead, the Father, Son and Holy Spirit. Each person in the Godhead would fulfill their part in the contract which involved creation and redemption. The eternal characteristics of the Godhead are thus stamped upon this covenant as well as all other covenants.

a. **The Father** is the originator of the covenants. He makes the promises; He gives the words and the terms of the covenants.

b. **The Son** is the sacrifice, the mediator of the covenant, functioning in the sanctuary as both offering and offerer, sacrifice and priest.

c. **The Holy Spirit** is the seal, the sign and the token. He is the person in the

Godhead who would be the executor of the covenant and see that it would be carried out in full.

The great doctrines of Foreknowledge, Election, Sovereign will of God, Purpose and Predestination all declare the language and truth of covenantal revelation in the Godhead in eternity and time (Romans 16:26; Psalms 106:48; 112:6; Habakkuk 1:12; Hebrews 13:20).

4.   **Eternal because it is Spiritual**

Only by understanding the Everlasting Covenant can we understand many of the "everlasting" promises spoken of in certain of the other covenants. Following are some of the most important factors about this covenant that illustrate its eternal value.

a.   It is the only covenant made in *eternity*, before time began.

b.   It is the covenant made in the counsels of the persons of the eternal Godhead. Man was not party to it but the object of it.

c.   It is the only *heavenly* covenant, all others pertaining to earth.

d.   It is the only covenant without temporal elements, for it involves, from the Divine point, the eternal persons in the Godhead, and for man it involves eternal life.

e.   It is the most comprehensive covenant for all others are but the progressive unfolding on earth and in time of that which is in the Everlasting Covenant.

f.   It is the fulfilment, by the New Covenant, of the "everlasting" elements of all other covenants. Earthly covenants generally had both temporal and everlasting elements in them. Most of the temporal elements were fulfilled and abolished at the cross, while the remaining temporal elements pass away at Christ's second coming. This is seen in the following examples:

(1)   The rainbow token belonged to the everlasting Noahic Covenant (Genesis 9:12,16). This can only be "everlasting" in Christ (Revelation 10:1).

(2)   The promised land was to be an "everlasting possession" to Abraham and his seed (Genesis 17:8; 48:26). This can only be in the heavenly Canaan, for the earth is to pass away with fervent heat (II Peter 3:3-10; Hebrews 11:10-16).

(3)   The rite of circumcision of the Abrahamic Covenant was to be an "everlasting token" in the flesh of Abraham's seed (Genesis 17:13). The physical token was but temporal and therefore the circumcision that is everlasting is of the heart and spirit, and therefore spiritual (Romans 2:28,29; Colossians 2:12; Galatians 6:15,16).

(4)   Certain of the rituals of the Mosaic Covenant were to be "everlasting" and "perpetual" (Leviticus 24:8; 16:34). All such were fulfilled and abolished at the cross. So it is the spiritual principle in these things that are eternal.

(5)   Aaron and his sons, Phinehas also, were promised "the covenant of an everlasting priesthood" (Exodus 40:12-15; Numbers 25:12,13). This could not be the Aaronic priesthood as Hebrews clearly show that the priesthood pertaining to the Mosaic Covenant was done away. Therefore, Phinehas could only receive the covenant of an everlasting priesthood through the New Covenant priesthood, after the order of Melchisedek. This is the

priesthood of Christ and His Church that lives on in the power of an endless life (Hebrews 7:16; Psalms 110; Revelation 1:6; 5:9,10; 20:6).

(6) The Lord promised the Levites that they would never lack priests to offer the continual sacrifices as His ministers (Jeremiah 33:17-22). However, the Epistle to the Hebrews tells us that the Levitical order and animal sacrifices of the Old Covenant are done away (Hebrews 7-8-9-10). Therefore these promises can only find fulfilment in a spiritual and eternal priesthood in the New Covenant priesthood and sacrifices (I Peter 2:5-9).

(7) The "everlasting" seed, house, throne and kingdom of the Davidic Covenant also can only find fulfilment in Christ, who is the seed of David, and in His house, throne and kingdom in the Church (II Samuel 23:5; Isaiah 55:3).

(8) All covenants which are spoken of as "everlasting" can only be such through the Everlasting Covenant made by the Godhead (Genesis 9:16; 17:7,19; II Samuel 23:5; I Chronicles 16:17; Psalms 105:10; Isaiah 24:5,6; 61:8; Jeremiah 32:40; Ezekiel 16:60; 37:27).

So it is with all "everlasting" promises in covenants of earth having both temporal and everlasting elements in them. The temporal elements flow to and are fulfilled and abolished at the cross, while everlasting elements flow through the cross into the New Covenant. The New Covenant with its promise of eternal life brings redeemed mankind into the Everlasting Covenant. The New Covenant makes possible the creative and redemptive parts of the Everlasting Covenant, bringing God and man together in covenantal relationship eternally. God counts the things that are not as though they were because of His attributes (Romans 4:17). As far as the believer in the New Covenant is concerned he is ushered into the Everlasting Covenant at the second coming of Christ.

I. **The WORDS of the Covenant**

The Scriptures show that God's foreknowledge, election, calling and predestined purposes took place both *before* the foundation of the world (John 17:5,24; Ephesians 1:4,9,11; 3:10,11; II Timothy 1:9,10; Ephesians 2:10; I Corinthians 2:7), as well as *from* the foundation of the world (Matthew 25:34; Revelation 13:8; 17:8). Numerous promises are given by God in the Bible. All are Yea and Amen in Christ Jesus (II Corinthians 1:20). Only the major promises are noted here.

A. **The Promises of the Covenant**

1. **Promises of Blessing**

a. **Everlasting Life**

The major promise of this covenant is the all-inclusive promise of eternal or everlasting life. This was promised by God, who cannot lie, before the world began (Titus 1:2,3; I John 2:25). It is the greatest promise that Jesus ever gave and it was made possible and available through the New Covenant (John 3:16,36; 4:14; 5:24; 6:27,40,47; 12:50; Acts 13:46; Romans 6:22; Matthew 19:29; Galatians 6:8; I Timothy 6:16; Luke 18:30; Daniel 12:2).

The words of the New Covenant are actually the words of the Everlasting Covenant which had been hid in God and later revealed by Christ (Deuteronomy 29:29; John 1:14-18; Romans 16:25,26; Ephesians 3:9-11).

b. **Immortality**

To have eternal life as God does also involves the promise of immortality (II Timothy 1:9,10; I Timothy 6:16; Romans 2:7; II Corinthians 5:1-5; I Corinthians 15:15-57). Mortality means death-doomed. Covenant promises make immortality available to man in Christ by which he will receive an immortal body, never to die, but to live in the power of eternal life.

c. **Everlasting Kingdom**

God's kingdom is an everlasting kingdom which the believer inherits. Having been taken out of the kingdom of darkness he now comes into the kingdom of life and light (Psalms 145:13; Matthew 25:34; I Corinthians 6:9,10; Ephesians 5:5; Galatians 5:21; II Peter 1:11; Daniel 4:3,34; 7:14,27).

d. **Eternal Inheritance**

That inheritance lost in Adam is restored in Christ (Hebrews 9:14).

e. **Everlasting Love, Kindness and Mercy**

Saved from everlasting judgment, the believer finds everlasting love, kindness and mercy from God through Christ (Jeremiah 31:3; Isaiah 54:8; Psalms 100:5; 103:17).

f. **Everlasting Righteousness**

Christ brought man an everlasting righteousness which he could never obtain of himself (Daniel 9:24).

g. **Everlasting Habitations**

The New Covenant believer will be received into everlasting dwelling-places (Luke 16:9).

h. **Everlasting Joy** (Isaiah 51:11; 61:7).

i. **Everlasting Strength** (Isaiah 26:4).

j. **Everlasting Name** (Isaiah 56:5; 63:12,16).

k. **Everlasting Promises to Overcomers**

Each of the promises to the overcomers involve eternal realities.

(1) The overcomer is given the tree of eternal life forfeited under the Edenic Covenant (Genesis 2:9,16,17; Revelation 2:7; 22:2,14).

(2) The overcomer is given the promise that he should not be hurt of the second death, which death began in Adam (Revelation 2:11 with Genesis 2:16,17; Revelation 21:4).

(3) The overcomer is further given the promise of hidden manna and a white stone with a new name in it. To eat of this manna one shall never die (Revelation 2:17; John 6:53-63).

(4) The overcomer is given the promise of power over the nations, ruling with a rod of iron. He is also given the morning star of light. It speaks of ruling and reigning with Jesus over all enemies (Revelation 2:26-28; 22:16).

(5) The overcomer is given the promise of being clothed with white

raiment and having his name confessed before the Father and the angels (Revelation 3:4,5). It will be the white raiment of light from his glorified body; that raiment which Adam and Eve lost in the Fall.

(6) The overcomer is given the promise of being a pillar in the temple of God and having the name of the Father, the name of the bride-city, and the Son's new name written upon him (Revelation 3:12). It speaks of the perfect nature, image and character of God in Christ upon them.

(7) The overcomer will inherit all things and God will be his God does in His Father's throne (Revelation 3:12). All the dominion lost in Adam is now restored in Christ.

(8) The overcome will inherit all things and God will be his God (Revelation 21:7). This is the promise of promises for it comprehends all the promises of God ever made. Those promises having eternal elements in them will be enjoyed for ever.

It should be noted that there are some promises in the Bible which can be appropriated and received here and now. There are other promises that believers never received on earth, but died in faith of such. These will be received in the eternities to come, in the eternal city of God (Hebrews 11:33,8-16,39; Titus 1:1,2; John 6:39,40,44,54; I John 2:25; Revelation 21-22).

The Bible has numerous promises for the redeemed and that which is "eternal" in them is made possible by the New Covenant in the Everlasting Covenant. All of the promises of redemption, salvation through grace, resurrection and eternal life were in the Everlasting Covenant and gradually unfolded in the earthly covenants, the fullest being the New Covenant and its promises.

2. Promises of Cursing

The curses of any of the earthly covenants find their consummation in the curse of the Everlasting Covenant. The greatest of all curses is to be banished from the presence of God and the Lamb rejected, and to be cast into the eternal Lake of Fire, the final Hell. This is the curse of curses. All who reject God's New Covenant in Christ, rejecting the words, the sacrifice and the seal of the covenant, are cast into Hell after the Great White Throne Judgment. This final Hell is spoken of as:

a. **Everlasting shame and contempt** (Daniel 12:2).

b. **Everlasting lake of fire and brimstone** (Matthew 18:8; Revelation 14:10,11; 19:20; 20:14,15; 21:8).

c. **Everlasting Punishment** (Matthew 25:41,46).

d. **Everlasting Destruction** (II Thessalonians 1:9).

e. **Everlasting chains of darkness** (Jude 6; II Peter 2:4). For sinful angels also.

f. **Perdition** (Revelation 17:8; I Timothy 6:9; John 17:12).

g. **The Second Death** (Revelation 2:11; 20:13-15; 21:8).

Those who go to this terrible place chose to reject God's redemptive covenant terms in Christ, and thus are eternally out of covenant relationship with God. They reject the "everlasting Gospel" (Revelation 14:6-11). Hell was not prepared for man but for the Devil and his angels. But all who make their "covenant with death and hell" (Isaiah 28:14,15,18,19) and serve the Devil and sin will live eternally with him in this prison. Such punishment and torment will last as long as eternal bliss does for those who have accepted God's covenant in Christ (Matthew 25:41,46).

B. **The Terms of the Covenant**

1. **Faith**

God's love for the world is demonstrated in the giving of His only begotten Son and whosoever believes on Him is given everlasting life (John 3:16; I Peter 1:19-20).

2. **Love**

In that love was God's motive in both creation and redemption it is entirely appropriate that man has a love response to God's loving initiative (I John 4:19; Jeremiah 31:3). If we love Him we will keep His commandments (John 14:15; 15:9,10; I John 3:22-24; 4:11-18; 5:2,3).

3. **Obedience**

Jesus Christ is the author of eternal salvation unto all them obey Him (Hebrews 5:9; Revelation 22:14).

Adam fell from faith and loving obedience under the Edenic Covenant. Through the New Covenant in Christ we are restored to that faith and obedience of love for all eternity. Such will be the terms of the Everlasting Covenant promises in the eternities to come.

God's ultimate intention in the creation of man was to bring man to a state of sinless perfection, from which it would be impossible to fall. This "making" process was interrupted by the fall of man, but it is through the full working of the New Covenant that God imparts His own sinless perfection to man ensuring his perfect faith and loving obedience for all eternity.

C. **The Oath of the Covenant**

In the counsels of the Godhead, the Father gave His Son His oath. This oath involved the fact that, upon the Son's incarnation and voluntary and substitutionary death for sin, the Father would raise Him from the dead and give to Him an eternal priesthood after the order of Melchisedek (Psalms 110:1-4; Hebrews 7:20-25; Acts 2:23-26).

The oath of the Noahic, Abrahamic, Davidic and New Covenants are but the expressions on earth of this oath of the Everlasting Covenant.

D. **The Book of the Covenant**

Because the Everlasting Covenant is based on the essential attributes of God, upon God's foreknowledge, elective and predestined purpose (Romans 8:28-30; 16:25,26; I Peter 1:1,2), God was able to place the names of the redeemed in

His book. It is spoken of as "the Lamb's book of life" (Revelation 13:8; 17:8; 3:5; 22:19; Exodus 32:32; Philippians 4:3; Revelation 20:12-15).

II. The BLOOD of the Covenant

Because the covenants of God involves both the creation and redemption of man, and because God foresaw the Fall of man, the Everlasting Covenant necessitated the incarnation of the eternal Son of God. It was this eternal purpose of God contained in the Everlasting Covenant that was fulfilled in the work of Christ in the New Covenant.

A. The Sacrifice of the Covenant

1. The Body

Man was made a triune being; spirit, soul and body. The fact of man's sin necessitated man's redemption. None of Adam's race could redeem as all are born in sin and shapen in iniquity. Hence it necessitated God to come and redeem man. But God could not redeem man as God only but God had to become man to redeem man. It was the Son of God who became man by taking on Himself a human body. The WORD was made flesh (John 1:1-3,14-18). The Son was God incarnate. By taking upon Himself a sinless human body, Jesus Christ made the supreme sacrifice for man's sin. All animal body sacrifices simply pointed to the sacrifice of the sinless body of Jesus offered once for all (Hebrews 9-10).

This virgin-born, sinless body was crucified on Calvary. Then after three days it was raised incorruptible, immortal and glorified. Jesus has this same glorified body in heaven at the Father's right hand and this becomes the surety of the New Covenant and the Everlasting Covenant. It is the covenant body of the eternal Son of God (Matthew 1:18-25; Luke 1:30-33; John 1:1-3,14-18; Hebrews 10:5-14; Romans 1:3; Galatians 4:4).

As such, He is the seed of the woman, and the seed of Abraham, Isaac and Jacob and David, after the flesh (Romans 9:5). As such He is the Lamb of God which taketh away the sin of the world (John 1:29,36).

2. The Blood

Because the blood is the life of man, and of all flesh, and man's blood became corrupted by the entrance of sin, sinless blood was needed to redeem man. Hence because "the children are partakers of flesh and blood" it was necessary that the eternal Son of God, by reason of the Everlasting Covenant, take upon Himself "flesh and blood" (Hebrews 2:14).

This also was done in the incarnation. The Holy Spirit over-shadowing the Virgin Mary planted within her the Divine seed of the Father and with it the sinless blood needed for the atonement.

The blood of Jesus was poured out as the cleansing agent for sin. This blood is sinless and therefore incorruptible. It is in heaven for us now and it is upon the throne of God. It is there as "the blood of the everlasting covenant" (Hebrews 13:20; 9:11-28; 10:29). All sacrificial animal blood under the Old Testament altars pointed to the blood of God in the blood of Christ (Acts 20:28; I John 1:7). Jesus Christ is the Lamb slain from the foundation of the world, as well as before that foundation (Revelation 13:8; 17:8; I Peter 1:19-20).

It is through this blood that, ultimately, an end will be made of sin, transgression will be finished, iniquity purged, and the heavens and earth shall be cleansed of the presence of Satan and his evil hosts (Revelation 12:4-12; Job 15:15; Hebrews 9).

B. **The Mediator of the Covenant**

1. **The Lord Jesus Christ**

In the counsels of the eternal Godhead, the Covenantors, the Son, as the central person was ordained to be the mediator as well as the sacrifice. The sacrifice of His sinless body and blood pertains to His perfect humanity. The priesthood and mediatorial ministry pertain to His deity. Thus human nature and Divine nature are brought together in Jesus Christ, the God-Man and the mediatorial person in the Godhead.

This priesthood is sworn by oath to be the priesthood for ever after the order of Melchisedek. Jesus Christ lives in the power of an endless life by the resurrection. Therefore there can never be a successor or change of His priesthood. All earthly priesthoods, patriarchal, Aaronic and Levitical, shadowed forth His priesthood. They were temporal; His is an eternal priesthood because of His eternal Sonship in the eternal Godhead. He is our Melchisedek, the King-Priest of the Abrahamic Covenant and fulfilled in the New Covenant (Genesis 14:18-20; Psalms 110; Hebrews 5-6-7; 8:6; 12:22-24). All of His Old Testament "goings forth" consummated in His incarnation to be our Saviour and Mediator under the New Testament (Micah 5:2; John 16:27,28).

2. **The Church**

Because the Everlasting Covenant pertained to the redemption of all who would believe and obey, it made possible a priestly body to be joined to the Redeemer, Jesus Christ. Hence, Christ and His Body, which is the Church, together constitute the priesthood after the order of Melchisedek.

The believers will be kings and priests unto God and His Christ eternally. This covenant of an everlasting priesthood is the one that Phinehas, and other priests and saints enter into, whether on this or the other side of the cross. Patriarchal, Aaronic and Levitical priesthoods and orders all shadowed the eternal priesthood of this order of Melchisedek (Revelation 1:6; 5:9,10; 20-6; Numbers 25:12,13; Acts 6:7; I Peter 2:5-9; Hebrews 5-6-7; Jeremiah 10:10).

It is "in Christ" that God sees the believer as a king-priest for ever after the order of Melchisedek, King of Righteousness and King of Peace (Ephesians 1:4,5,9,11; 3:11).

C. **The Sanctuary of the Covenant**

The Scriptures clearly state that there is an heavenly sanctuary, tabernacle or temple. It is the archetype, the prototype or the original sanctuary. The earthly sanctuaries of other covenants were only the shadows on earth of the true and heavenly sanctuary which the Lord pitched and not man (Revelation 15:5-8; 11:19).

Again, all the ministry in earthly sanctuaries only shadowed forth Christ's ministry "within the veil" of the heavenly sanctuary. The Book of Hebrews especially deals with the sacrifice, the priesthood and the sanctuary of Christ

(Hebrews 6:19,20; 8:1-5; 9:11,12,24; Isaiah 66:1-4; Acts 7:48-50; I Kings 8:27).

The ultimate and eternal "tabernacle of God" and the dwelling place of the redeemed will be the heavenly city, New Jerusalem. In it is the throne of God and the Lamb, the Covenantors of the Everlasting Covenant (Revelation 21-22). It is this city that Abraham, Isaac and Jacob looked for, a city having foundations, whose builder and maker is God (Hebrews 11:10-16; 12:22-24; 13:14; II Peter 3:8-10; Isaiah 60:19,20). It is situated on the New Heavens and New Earth.

III. The SEAL of the Covenant

There are two aspects to the seal of the Everlasting Covenant; that which pertains to God and that which pertains to man.

1. The Seal of the Holy Spirit

When the Everlasting Covenant was made in the counsels of the Godhead, the blessed Holy Spirit, the third person in the Godhead, was ordained to be the sign, seal and token of this covenant. With the promises of the Father, the sacrifice of the Son, the Holy Spirit Himself would be the executor of the covenant. Hence the Holy Spirit is spoken of as:

a. The Promise of the Father (Luke 24:49; Acts 2:39).

b. The Spirit of Promise (Ephesians 1:13,14).

c. The Seal (Ephesians 1:13,14; 4:20; II Corinthians 1:22).

d. The Earnest (II Corinthians 1:22).

e. The Firstfruits (Romans 8:23).

The Holy Spirit Himself as the seal of the New Covenant, as the Earnest, and as the Firstfruits points to the completeness of the seal and work of the Spirit which takes place under entrance into the Everlasting Covenant. This complete work pertains to the other part of the seal as it pertains to man.

2. The Seal of the Glorified Body

a. Pertaining to Christ

The bodily resurrection and glorification of Christ's humanity, His virgin-born, sinless and crucified body, by the power of the Holy Spirit, became the seal of the Everlasting Covenant (Romans 1:1-4; Hebrews 13:20). In the Godhead counsels in the Everlasting Covenant, it was agreed that, upon the Son's completed sacrifice for sin and His burial in the tomb for three days and three nights, the Holy Spirit would raise Him from the dead. The Spirit would quicken the body of Jesus to life and glory to live in the power of an endless life (Hebrews 7:16). This body would be the same body but spiritual and glorious. It would be the *seal of the Spirit* upon the accepted and finished work of Christ (Romans 8:11; Acts 2:23-26; Romans 7:4; Ephesians 1:13-23; Philippians 3:21; Romans 1:1-4).

In His ascension, Jesus took this virgin-born, sinless, crucified and now glorified body back into heaven. There is a glorified Man in the Godhead. His glorified body has become the surety, the token and seal of that which the Holy Spirit will do for all believers in the consummation of covenantal promises (Hebrews 7:22).

The glorious spiritual body cannot be separated from the power of the Holy Spirit. The Holy Spirit will quicken our mortal bodies as He quickened Christ's body (Romans 8:10,11).

b. **Pertaining to the Church**

As pertaining to the believer, the final and complete aspect of the seal of God is the immortalization and glorification of his redeemed body (II Timothy 1:9,10; I Timothy 6:16; Romans 2:7; 8:9-11; Titus 1:2).

That the believer is redeemed spiritually by the New Covenant is noted by many Scriptures. He is "born of the Spirit" and "sealed by the Spirit" (John 3:1-5; Romans 8:16,17; II Corinthians 1:22; Ephesians 1:13,14; 4:30). However, the Scriptures also show that the final redemption that the believer will experience is that which pertains to the *physical body.* We groan within ourselves, waiting for the redemption of our body (Romans 8:22-25; I Corinthians 6:19,20; Luke 21:28).

When Christ comes the second time, the dead in Christ are raised first and the living believers are changed. Together they receive an immortalized and glorified body. All believers will receive a glorified body like unto Christ's glorious body (Philippians 3:20,21). The promise is the ultimate of that which was promised and made possible by the New Covenant (II Corinthians 5:1-5; I Corinthians 15:51-57. I Thessalonians 4:15-18; Philippians 3:20,21; John 11:24-27). This will indeed be the seal of God upon those in covenantal relationship with Him through Christ.

The resurrected and immortalized bodies of the saints will shine in the varied glories of the sun, moon and stars; all will shine as light (I Corinthians 15:35-50). This takes place at Christ's coming, at the last trump. This ushers the believer, by the New Covenant, into eternity and the complete benefits of the Everlasting Covenant made in eternity past before time began (Ephesians 1:1-12; 2:7; 3:9-12).

The "sample" glorious body is the body of Christ (Philippians 3:20,21). The Man in the Godhead is our surety of the full and complete seal (Hebrews 7:22; Luke 24:36-40; I John 1:1-3; John 1:14-18).

All seals of previous covenants flowed to the cross and pointed to the New Covenant seal, the Holy Spirit. The New Covenant seal of the covenantal name in baptism and the Holy Spirit of God point to and make possible the completeness of the seal of the Everlasting Covenant; the redemption, immortalization and glorification of the believer's body.

The New Covenant seal is but the earnest, the foretaste, the firstfruits of the Spirit's work. The completion of the Spirit's work is the glorified body; a spiritual, yet real and eternal body like Christ's.

The Holy Spirit and the spiritual body together, therefore, constitute the seal, sign and token of the Everlasting Covenant for the redeemed of all ages, those redeemed out of every kindred, tongue, tribe and nation. In terrible contrast there will be those who have rejected the covenants of God, rejected Christ and thus forfeit their bodies in Hell fire and suffer spiritual torments for eternity (Mark 9:43-49; Matthew 10:28).

It is because of the work of the Spirit to be completed in the redemption of the believer's body that the New Covenant person will seek to glorify God in his spirit and body for he has been bought with a great price (I Corinthians 6:19,20).

Chapter 11

THE COVENANTAL NAME

Relative to any covenant is that which pertains to the person or persons entering into covenant and that is the name or the names of the covenanters. Henry D. Houghton says that most human covenants have five distinct and essential elements to them; these elements being the following:

1. The **DATE** of the agreement.

2. The **PARTIES** between whom the covenant is made.

3. The **SUBJECT** or scope of the covenant.

4. The **TIME** and operation of the agreement, limited or otherwise.

5. The **SIGNATURE**, i.e. the Person's name.

The same is true of the Divine Covenants. Each of the Divine covenants are stamped with God's Time upon them, the Parties involved, the Subject and scope of the covenantal word, the Time and operation of the covenant, being either temporal or everlasting, and finally signed with the Name of God.

When the covenant had been drawn up and the parties involved entered into covenant by sacrifice, the contract was signed with the person's names. Some customs of certain tribes signed their name in blood. The name was also used as a seal of the covenant. A covenant was only as good as the person's name. The covenant was invalid without the persons signature.

When it comes to the Divine covenants, which fall basically into two groupings, the name of God is indelibly stamped upon each. This name also becomes God's seal as to the authenticity of His covenants. Because of Christ's work at Calvary, the Divine covenants have indeed been "signed in blood", the blood of the Lord Jesus Christ.

The two groupings of Divine covenants have to do with the Covenant of Creation and the Covenants of Redemption. Because this is so, the Bible reveals two groupings of Divine Names and/or Titles; these Names or Titles having to do with Creation and those having to do with Redemption.

It is because God has signed His name to His covenants that He often moved in behalf of His people, in spite of their wickedness "for His Name's sake" (Ezekiel 20:9,14, 22,39,44).

A. The Elohistic Names of God — The Covenant of Creation.

The first covenant involving man is the Edenic Covenant, the covenant of creation, revealing God's purpose for man. This covenant is signed with the name of God, involving the persons of the Godhead, even the Father, Son and Holy Spirit. Genesis

1 uses the title or name "GOD" about 32 times. The Hebrew word "Elohim" is a Hebrew uni-plural word denoting the unity in plurality of the Divine Persons. The word "Elohim" simply means "object, or objects of worship". Throughout the Scripture it is used of the true God, of angels, of devils and even of men (Psalms 82:1; 138:1; I Corinthians 8:4-6; John 10:33-35).

"El" in the singular means "The Strong One, The Mighty One". "Elohim" in the uni-plural form involves the three persons in the Godhead, the Covenanters. God said in the covenant of creation, "Let US make man in OUR image, after OUR likeness" and "God created man in HIS own image, in the image of God He made them". It was ELOHIM speaking (Genesis 1:26-28). The Divine Covenanters, Father, Son and Holy Spirit, were active in this Edenic Covenant, declaring the purpose for the creation of man.

The Elohistic Name of God is used thousands of times in the Bible. Its prominent truth is that God is the Creator, the Strong One, the Mighty One and the one and only true object of worship for man, the creature. Man was created to worship God, the Creator, for he owes and depends upon God for his very existence. He was created to glorify and worship God and to do His will (Matthew 4:10; Deuteronomy 6:13; 10:20; Revelation 4:11).

Wherever the Elohistic name or title is used in Scripture it always speaks of God the creator and pertains to the covenant of creation, the Edenic Covenant in particular. The various Elohistic names are generally translated as "God". Following are some of the compound Elohistic names or titles of God, along with the singular use of the same. When a compound name is used, it is generally using the creatorship name with one or more of the attributes of God.

1. **El** — The Strong One, The Mighty One, the Creator.

   It is used of the Godhead in the singular, showing that each person in the Godhead is God, co-equal in nature, power, attributes and glory

   * The Father is El (Genesis 14:18-22).
   * The Son is El (Isaiah 7:14; 9:6; Psalms 22:1; 89:26).
   * The Holy Spirit is El (Job 33:4; 37:10).

2. **Elohim** — God or Gods, The Strong One, the Mighty One. It is the Old Testament equivalent to the New Testament Father, Son and Holy Spirit. It speaks of unity yet plurality in the Divine Persons (Genesis 1:1-26).

3. **Eloah** — The One and only true God, in contrast to the polytheistic and pantheistic religions of heathen nations. It speaks of the unity of God's being (Deuteronomy 32:15; Daniel 2:11).

4. **El-Elyon** — God, the Most High. It signifies the omnipresence of God, who is high above all things (Genesis 14:19).

5. **El-Shaddai** — God Almighty, The Strong One, the Breasted One, the All-Sufficient One. It involves the omnipotence of His being (Genesis 17:1).

6. **El-Roi** — God, the All-seeing, the God who sees me. It speaks of the omniscience of His being (Genesis 16:13,14).

7. **El-Olam** — God, the Everlasting God. It signifies eternity of being (Genesis 21:33).

8. **El-Bethel** — God of the House of God. It signifies the revelation of His being in His dwelling place (Genesis 28:19; 31:13).

9. **El-Elohe-Israel** — God, the God of the Prince having power with God and man. The God of Jacob whose name was changed to Israel. He is the God who changes human names and human nature to partake of His name and His nature (Genesis 33:20).

    These compound Elohistic names or titles of God use the signature of God who is a covenant keeping God as the God of creation.

10. **El-Gibbor** — The Mighty or Great God (Isaiah 9:6; Jeremiah 32:18,19).

11. **Elohim-Elyon** — God, The Most High (Psalms 91:1,2; 78:56).

12. **Elohim-Saboath** — God of Hosts (Psalms 80:7,14).

13. **Adon** or **Adonai** — Master, Owner(s), Ruler of all (Psalms 147:5; 86:12).

14. **Immanu-El** — God with us.

    The greatest of all these Elohistic names is revealed in the name Immanu-El, which means "GOD with us" (Isaiah 7:14; Matthew 1:21-23). All the compound Elohistic names of God consummate in this name. Jesus Christ is God incarnate, God made flesh, the Incarnate Word, the new creation. The previous creation of man in Eden pointed to the new creation in redemption, of which Jesus Christ is the beginning (John 1:13,14-18; Revelation 3:14).

B.   **The Jehovahistic Names of God — The Covenants of Redemption**

All of the subsequent covenants revealed in the Bible are covenants of redemption's plan. Each is signed with the dominant redemptive name of God, as well as, many times, linked in compound significance with the name of God in the covenant of creation.

When this is seen, Creation and Redemption are brought together, for the God who creates man is also the God who redeems man.

The clearest revelation of the redemptive covenantal name of God is given for us in the call of God to Moses at the burning bush and in the process of Israel's deliverance from Egypt's bondage. This is found in Exodus 3:1-15; 6:1-6.

When the Lord called Moses to deliver Israel from Egypt it was on the basis of the covenant made with Abraham, Isaac and Jacob (Exodus 2:23-25; 3:1-6). Moses, knowing that the Egyptians worshipped many gods, wanted to know by what name of the true God would he deliver Israel. Moses said to God "Behold when I come unto the children of Israel, and shall say unto them, The God of your fathers hath sent me unto you; and they shall say unto me, *What is His name?* What shall I say unto them" (Exodus 3:13).

God told Moses in time that He would judge all the gods of Egypt (Exodus 12:12). The name of God would be a name above all the gods of Egypt. God's reply to Moses question is found in Exodus 3:14,15. "And God said unto Moses, *I AM THAT I AM:*

and He said, Thus shalt thou say unto the children of Israel, *I AM* hath sent me unto you. And God said moreover unto Moses, Thus shalt thou say unto the children of Israel, the *LORD GOD* of your fathers, the God of Abraham, the God of Issac, and the God of Jacob, hath sent me unto you: *this is My name forever,* and this is My memorial unto all generations."

In Exodus 6:1-6 God further told Moses that He was not known (i.e., understood fully, or fully revealed in power) by His name JEHOVAH to Abraham, Isaac and Jacob, with whom He had made covenant. This is not to say that the covenantal name was not used in Genesis, but the full power of it was not manifested as it would be in the redemption of Israel from Egypt's house of bondage. The covenantal name of God in relation to redemption is revealed as JEHOVAH (Or, YAHWEH, and translated LORD above 6000 times in Scripture). When He signs the covenant He says "I am the Lord" (Exodus 6:2-8). Redemption is founded on grace and grace is manifested in covenant, signed by His redemptive name.

These are three major truths to be noted in connection with this name of God relative to the covenants of redemption.

1. **The Being of God**

   When God spoke to Moses out of the burning bush and declared His name, the first thing we see is that which pertains to the very nature and being of God. This is seen in the following:

   a. It is God or ELOHIM who speaks out of the bush. That is, the triunity of God's being is seen there, as Father, Son and Holy Spirit. He also identified Himself with men who represented His triune characteristics when He said that He was the God of Abraham, the God of Isaac and the God of Jacob. It is the covenanters in the Godhead who speak to Moses.

   b. When God declared His name to be *I AM THAT I AM,* He also expressed by this His essential attributes.

      * *I AM THAT I AM* expressed *eternity of being,* comprehending time past, time present and time future; that is, timelessness (Revelation 1:4).

      * *I AM THAT I AM* expresses *Self-existence,* that is, He is the life-source, depending on nothing and no-one outside Himself for His very existence (John 1:1-4; Acts 17:28).

      * *I AM THAT I AM* expresses the *essential attributes* of God such as omnipotence, (All-powerful); omnipresence (All-present) and omniscience (All-knowing and All-seeing).

The God of covenant reveals Himself as Father, Son and Holy Spirit and signs His name to His covenants. Because of His very being and His attributes He is able to make and fulfill His covenants. This is what is implicitly seen in the name LORD GOD or JEHOVAH ELOHIM, the I AM THAT I AM!

2. **The Activity of God**

   When God spoke to Moses and said His name was the LORD GOD, it also involved the meaning that He was a God who was active in behalf of His people. Jehovah's name (Or Yahweh, translated most often as Lord) means *"I will be what I will be"*. It declares the activity of God. It shows that God will be all that is necessary to His covenant people as their needs arise.

This name signifies the active presence of God the covenant-maker and covenant-keeper in behalf of His own. He is not just a God who exists as a being for Himself, but a God who is active in covenantal power.

This thought is particularly expressed to Moses in Exodus 6:1-6 when God says He will rid Israel, His covenant people, of the Egyptians by His mighty power and judgments. The plagues on Egypt showed God to be active in redemptive and covenantal power for His people, Israel.

3.   **The Redeeming and Creating Power of God**

The predominant truth in the name revealed to Moses in the bush is that which pertains to covenant. God remembered His covenant with Abraham, Isaac and Jacob (Exodus 2:24). The Abrahamic Covenant was a covenant of grace, an irrevocable covenant, and on this basis God would deliver His covenant nation. He did not exist in abstract or inactive sense for Himself, but to redeem His own. The covenant of redemption is involved. The *LORD* is the redemptive name, the covenantal name, and the power of the covenantal name would be fully seen in Egypt's judgments and Israel's deliverance (Exodus 6:3; 6:10; Romans 9:17).

Numerous are the times when God signs His name in covenantal truth: "The LORD is My Name" (Psalms 83:18; Isaiah 12:2; Malachi 3:6; Jeremiah 16:21); Isaiah 42:8).

When God combines His name in the LORD GOD, He gives us the combined truths of Redemption and Creation.

*   JEHOVAH — The Lord, The Covenant Redeemer.

*   Elohim — God, The Covenant Creator.

Redemption and Creation are brought together in the name of the LORD God, which is used thousands of times in the Bible.

Just as the Elohistic names of God, which are used in compound manner, so in the Jehovahistic names of God we see many compound redemptive names. In the Elohistic names of God, the compound name is generally linked with some essential attribute of God. But, in the Jehovahistic names of God, the compound name is generally associated with the needs of man, which can only be met by the God of Covenant, the God of redemption.

C.

Compound Redemptive Names

Following are the majority of the compound redemptive names of the God of covenant, the God of creation and the God of redemption. These compound Creator-Redeemer or Redeemer-Creator names were revealed to men in covenantal relationship with the Lord God and may be grouped accordingly.

1.   **Jehovah-Elohim** — The Lord God, the Redeemer-Creator (Genesis 2:4).

2.   **Jah** — Abbreviated form of Jehovah (Exodus 15:2; 17:16; Psalms 68:4).

3.   **Jehovah-Elohim-Saboath** — Lord God of Hosts. That is, of the hosts of heaven, creation and creatures (Psalms 84:8; Jeremiah 15:16).

4. **Adonai-Jehovah-Saboath** — Master, Lord of Hosts (Psalms 69:6).

5. **Jah-Jehovah** — Lord Jehovah (for double emphasis) (Isaiah 12:2; 26:4).

6. **Jah-Elohim** — Lord God (Psalms 68:18).

7. **Jehovah-Jireh** — The Lord will provide (Genesis 22:14).

8. **Jehovah-Rapha** — The Lord that heals (Exodus 15:26).

9. **Jehovah-Nissi** — The Lord my Banner (Exodus 17:15).

10. **Jehovah-Kanna** — The Lord who is Jealous (Exodus 20:5; 34:14; Deuteronomy 5:9).

11. **Jehovah-Mekaddeskum** — The Lord who sanctifies (Exodus 31:13; Leviticus 20:8).

12. **Jehovah-Shalom** — The Lord our Peace (Judges 6:24).

13. **Jehovah-Shaphat** — The Lord is Judge (Judges 11:27).

14. **Jehovah-Saboath** — The Lord of Hosts (I Samuel 1:3; Psalms 24:10; 84:1-3).

15. **Jehovah-Elyon** — The Lord Most High (Psalms 7:17).

16. **Jehovah-Raah** — The Lord my Shepherd (Psalms 23:1).

17. **Jehovah-Hosenu** — The Lord our Maker (Psalms 95:6).

18. **Jehovah-Gibbor** — The Lord is Mighty (Isaiah 42:13).

19. **Jehovah-Tsidkenu** — The Lord our Righteousness (Jeremiah 23:6).

20. **Jehovah-Shammah** — The Lord is There, or Everpresent (Ezekiel 48:35).

Each of these names may be grouped under their particular covenants, from the Edenic, Adamic, Abrahamic, Mosaic and to the Davidic Covenants. However, the greatest compound redemptive name ever to be revealed in this world or the world to come is the name of the *LORD JESUS CHRIST* (Matthew 1:21; Acts 2:34-36; Ephesians 1:19-23).

The Lord Jesus Christ is the New Covenant redeemer and all covenants pointed to Him. Because all the fulness of the Godhead bodily dwells in Him, it is fitting that all of the compound redemptive names of former covenants find fulfilment in Him who is the New Covenant personified and in whom is the greatest of all compound redemptive covenant names.

As the Godhead was involved in the Old Testament covenantal redemptive name of the *LORD GOD,* so the Godhead is involved in the New Covenant redemptive name of the *LORD JESUS CHRIST,* Jehovah's Saviour Anointed and the New Covenant name.

The triune Covenanters of the Everlasting Covenant share the triune name previously hidden in the counsels of the Godhead but revealed in the New Covenant.

When the *Father* gave the *words,* and the *Son* made the *sacrifice,* and the *Holy Spirit sealed* the New Covenant, all were signed with the redemptive name of the *Lord Jesus Christ.* The New Covenant is valid, signed by the name of the triune God.

Under the Mosaic Covenant, and even under succeeding covenants, the people of God often became partakers of the name of God with whom they were in covenantal relationship.

Under the Aaronic priesthood especially the covenantal name was invoked in a thrice-fold manner upon the Israelites in blessing (Numbers 6:22-27). The Israelites were a people called by His name (II Chronicles 7:14). Because they were in covenantal relationship with the Lord God they were partakers of the covenant name. For this reason they were forbidden to take the name of the Lord their God in vain, otherwise they would be guilty (Exodus 20:7; Ezekiel 20:12).

Because the believer in Christ is under the New Covenant, he also is in covenantal relationship with God through Christ, by the Spirit, and thus partakes of the triune covenantal and great redemptive name of the Lord Jesus Christ. The name of the Lord Jesus Christ is the greatest compound redemptive name ever to be revealed because it comprehends the greatest, even the name of the Godhead, the name of the Father, the Son and the Holy Spirit. It is also the greatest compound redemptive name because it comprehends in a triune name all previous redemptive names of all previous covenants. The New Covenant is the greatest of all covenants; so is the New Covenant name.

A person takes the New Covenant name, the redemptive name of the Lord Jesus Christ when he accepts the words of the covenant, the sacrifice of the covenant, and the seal of the covenant. The early believers were added to the Church, the covenant community by obeying the terms of the New Covenant. That is, they became members by repentance, faith, water baptism into the Godhead name and the baptism of the Holy Spirit.

This becomes the signature of the covenant God upon His New Covenant people. Those who are in covenantal relationship with God through Christ and upon whom the covenant name has been called are to depart from all iniquity (II Timothy 2:19). Read also Matthew 28:18-20; Mark 16:15-20; Acts 2:1-47; 11:26; Ephesians 1:13,14; Revelation 3:12; 7:1-3; 14:1; 22:4.

The name of the Lord Jesus Christ is the greatest redemptive name ever to be revealed because it comprehends in a triune name all the compound redemptive names of Jehovah. It is in the name and the person the Lord Jesus Christ that God meets every need of man in redemptive power. The Lord Jesus Christ is God's ordained covenant Redeemer and all Old Testament redemptive names point to and find their consummation in His redemptive name. It is the name of the Godhead bodily. It is a triune name for the triune God. It is the name of the God of covenant.

We may say with the Psalmist *"He will ever be mindful of His Covenant . . . He sent redemption unto His people: He hath commanded His Covenant for ever: holy and reverend is His Name"* (Psalms 111:5,9.).

. . . . . AMEN . . . . .

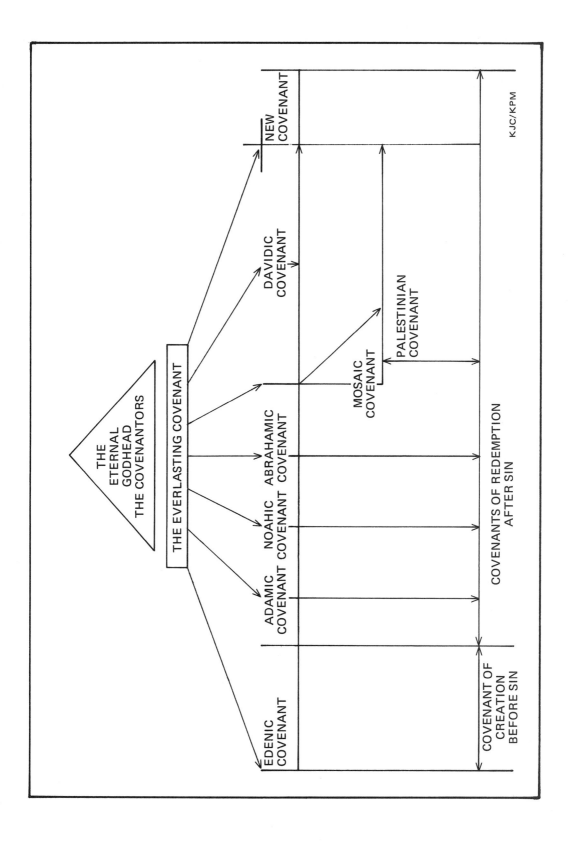

THE ETERNAL GODHEAD THE COVENANTORS

THE EVERLASTING COVENANT

EDENIC COVENANT

ADAMIC COVENANT

NOAHIC COVENANT

ABRAHAMIC COVENANT

MOSAIC COVENANT

PALESTINIAN COVENANT

DAVIDIC COVENANT

NEW COVENANT

COVENANT OF CREATION BEFORE SIN

COVENANTS OF REDEMPTION AFTER SIN

KJC/KPM

BIBLIOGRAPHY

1. Allen, J. H., *Judah's Sceptre and Joseph's Birthright,* Destiny Publishers, Merrimac, Mass., 1917.

2. Arndt, W. F. and Gingrich, F. W., *A Greek-English Lexicon of the New Testament.* The University of Chicago Press, Chicago, 60637, U.S.A., Zondervan Publishing House Edition, 1952.

3. Conner, Kevin J., *The Foundations of Christian Doctrine,* Portland, Oregon, Bible Press, U.S.A., 1980.

4. Conner, Kevin J., *The Name of God,* Portland, Oregon, Bible Press, U.S.A., 1975.

5. Conner, Kevin J. and Malmin, Kenneth P., *Interpreting the Scriptures,* Portland, Oregon, U.S.A., Bible Press, 1976.

6. Conner, Kevin J., *The Feasts of Israel,* Portland, Oregon, U.S.A., Bible Press, 1980.

7. Duty, Guy, *God's Covenants and Our Time,* Minneapolis, Minnesota, U.S.A., Bethany Press, Inc., 1964.

8. Gesenius, William, *A Hebrew and English Lexicon,* Oxford, Claredon Press, 1974.

9. Girdlestone, R. B., *Synonyms of the Old Testament,* Grand Rapids, Michigan, Wm. B. Eerdmans Publishing Company, 1973 Edition.

10. Kenyon, E. W., *The Blood Covenant,* Fullerton, California, U.S.A., Kenyon's Gospel Publishing Society, 1949.

11. Murray, Andrew, *The Two Covenants,* London, James Nisbet & Co. Ltd., 1898.

12. Moulton & Milligan, *Vocabulary of the Greek Testament.*

13. Pink, A. W., *The Divine Covenants,* Grand Rapids, Michigan, Baker Book House, 1973.

14. Strong, James, *Strong's Exhaustive Concordance,* New Jersey, Madison, 1890.

15. Thayer, Joseph Henry, D. D., *Thayer's Greek-English Lexicon,* Grand Rapids, Michigan, Associated Publishers & Authors Inc., 1885.

16. Trumbull, H. Clay, *The Blood Covenant,* Oakland, California, U.S.A., Bible House, 1975 Edition.

17. Vine, W. E., *An Expository Dictionary of New Testament Words,* Old Tappan, New Jersey, Fleming H. Revell Company, 1966.

Other Resources Available by Ken Malmin and Kevin Conner

Kevin J. Conner & Ken Malmin

The Covenants
Interpreting the Scriptures
New Testament Survey
Old Testament Survey

Ken Malmin

Bible Research

Kevin J. Conner

Church in the New Testament
The Book of Acts
Interpreting the Book of Revelation
Interpreting the Symbols & Types
Feasts of Israel
Foundations of Christian Doctrine
The Tabernacle of Moses
The Tabernacle of David
The Temple of Solomon

Ask for these resources at your local Christian bookstore.

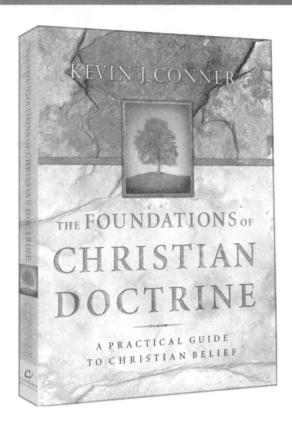

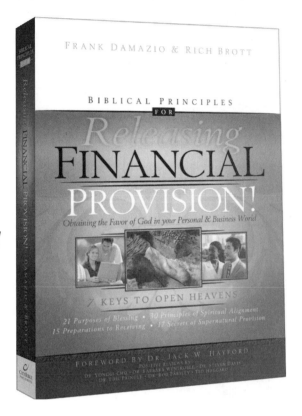

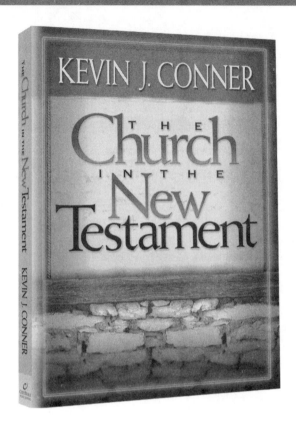

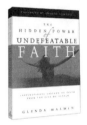

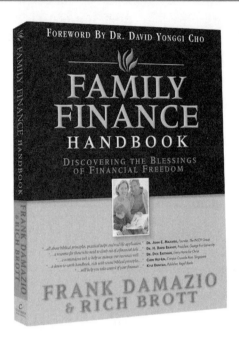

FAMILY FINANCE HANDBOOK

Discovering the Blessings of Financial Freedom

Frank Damazio & Rich Brott

With insights gained from twenty-five years in business and ministry, the authors impart to the reader biblical principles of stewardship and financial management. Readers learn how to get out of debt and are carefully guided through the investment process in this comprehensive and well-crafted resource.

Family Life / Finance / Christian Living

Softcover, 288 pages, 7 ½" X 10"
0-914936-60-3

"The Family Finance Handbook from Rich Brott and Frank Damazio provides a well-informed financial and stewardship guide for the individual, classroom, small group, and church stewardship presentation. It's all about biblical principles, practical helps and real life application."

DR. JOHN C. MAXWELL
Founder, The INJOY Group

"I pray that our Heavenly Father will abundantly bless your family with financial health through the reading of this book, so that you may also bless others for His glory."

DR. DAVID YONGGI CHO
Senior Pastor, Yoido Full Gospel Church, Seoul, Korea

"Although it is true that the joy of the Lord is our strength, nothing can rob us of that joy more than financial difficulty. The *Family Finance Handbook* is a tremendous tool to help us manage our resources well and thus stay joyfully strong in Jesus."

DR. DICK EASTMAN
International President, Every Home for Christ

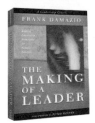
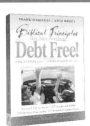

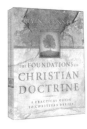

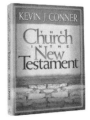
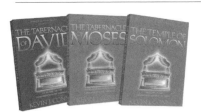

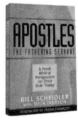